Neighborhoods and Intimate Partner Violence

Emily M. Wright

LFB Scholarly Publishing LLC
El Paso 2011

Copyright © 2011 by LFB Scholarly Publishing LLC

All rights reserved.

Library of Congress Cataloging-in-Publication Data

Wright, Emily M.
  Neighborhoods and intimate partner violence / Emily M. Wright.
       p. cm.
  Includes bibliographical references and index.
  ISBN 978-1-59332-437-7 (hbk. : alk. paper)
 1. Intimate partner violence. 2. Neighborhoods--Psychological aspects. 3. Neighborhoods--Social aspects. 4. Violence--Forecasting. I. Title.
  HV6626.W75 2010
  362.82'92--dc22
                                                          2010034263

ISBN 978-1-59332-437-7

Printed on acid-free 250-year-life paper.

Manufactured in the United States of America.

Criminal Justice
Recent Scholarship

Edited by
Marilyn McShane and Frank P. Williams III

A Series from LFB Scholarly

TABLE OF CONTENTS

LIST OF TABLES	vii
ACKNOWLEDGEMENTS	ix
CHAPTER ONE: The Importance of Intimate Partner Violence and Neighborhoods	1
CHAPTER TWO: Individual- and Couple-Level Predictors of Intimate Partner Violence	9
CHAPTER THREE: Social Disorganization Theory	27
CHAPTER FOUR: A Multi-Level Investigation of Intimate Partner Violence and Neighborhoods	61
CHAPTER FIVE: Neighborhood Influences on Intimate Partner Violence	91
CHAPTER SIX: Theoretical and Policy Implications	123
APPENDIX A	147
APPENDIX B	149
REFERENCES	151
INDEX	165

LIST OF TABLES

Table 1: Descriptive Statistics	69
Table 2: Random Coefficients model Predicting the Prevalence of IPV	93
Table 3: Level-Two (Structural Characteristics) Main Effects on the Prevalence of IPV (Level-One Intercepts as Outcomes)	95
Table 4: Level-Two (Collective Efficacy) Main Effects on the Prevalence of IPV (Level-One Intercepts as Outcomes)...	97
Table 5: Level-Two (Social Network Interaction) Main Effects on the Prevalence of IPV (Level-One Intercepts as Outcomes)	98
Table 6: Level-Two (Social Ties) Main Effects on the Prevalence of IPV (Level-One Intercepts as Outcomes)..	99
Table 7: Level-Two (Tolerance for Deviance) Main Effects on the Prevalence of IPV (Level-One Intercepts as Outcomes)	101
Table 8: Level-Two (Legal Cynicism) Main Effects on the Prevalence of IPV (Level-One Intercepts as Outcomes)..	102
Table 9: Level-Two (Satisfaction with Police) Main Effects on the Prevalence of IPV (Level-One Intercepts as Outcomes)	103
Table 10: Level-Two (Physical Disorder) Main Effects on the Prevalence of IPV (Level-One Intercepts as Outcomes)....	104
Table 11: Level-Two (Social Disorder) Main Effects on the Prevalence of IPV (Level-One Intercepts as Outcomes)..	106
Table 12: Random Coefficients model Predicting the Incidence of IPV...	109
Table 13: Level-Two (Structural Characteristics) Main Effects on the Incidence of IPV (Level-One Intercepts as Outcomes)	110
Table 14: Level-Two (Collective Efficacy) Main Effects on the Incidence of IPV (Level-One Intercepts as Outcomes)	111

Table 15: Level-Two (Social Network Interaction) Main
Effects on the Incidence of IPV (Level-One Intercepts as
Outcomes) 113
Table 16: Level-Two (Social Ties) Main Effects on the
Incidence of IPV (Level-One Intercepts as
Outcomes)... 114
Table 17: Level-Two (Tolerance for Deviance) Main Effects
on the Incidence of IPV (Level-One Intercepts as
Outcomes) 115
Table 18: Level-Two (Legal Cynicism) Main Effects on the
Incidence of IPV (Level-One Intercepts as
Outcomes)... 116
Table 19: Level-Two (Satisfaction with Police) Main Effects
on the Incidence of IPV (Level-One Intercepts as
Outcomes) 118
Table 20: Level-Two (Physical Disorder) Main Effects on the
Incidence of IPV (Level-One Intercepts as
Outcomes)... 119
Table 21: Level-Two (Social Disorder) Main Effects on the
Incidence of IPV (Level-One Intercepts as
Outcomes)... 120
Table 22: Summary of Main Results............................... 122

viii

ACKNOWLEDEGEMENTS

I am grateful to Drs. Michael Benson, Frank Cullen, Pam Wilcox, and D. Wayne Osgood for their guidance during the early writing of this book. I am also very appreciative of my family's support and understanding throughout this process. Finally, I would like to thank my husband, Benjamin Steiner, for his encouragement and patience.

CHAPTER ONE

The Importance of Intimate Partner Violence and Neighborhoods

Most people believe that strangers present the greatest threat of criminal perpetration. The reality, however, is that we are just as likely to be victimized in our own homes, "behind closed doors," and by our loved ones as we are to be attacked on the street by strangers (Gelles & Straus, 1988). In fact, the National Violence Against Women (NVAW) Survey estimates that approximately 1.5 million women and over 800,000 men are victimized by intimate partner violence every year (Tjaden & Thoennes, 1998).

In 2008, females were victimized by over 550,000 rape or sexual assaults, robbery, or aggravated or simple assaults by an intimate partner, while men were victimized by approximately 100,000 such acts (Catalano, Smith, Snyder, & Rand, 2009). The risk for women also increases over their lifetimes – it is estimated that over 22 percent of women will be physically assaulted by an intimate partner at some point in their lives (Tjaden & Thoennes, 1998). Although intimate partner violence most likely results in nonfatal injuries, the violence that occurs between partners can also be lethal. To demonstrate, intimate partners committed 14 percent of all homicides in the United States in 2007 (Catalano et al., 2009). Females are twice as likely to be killed by intimates as males. In 2007, 70 percent of intimate homicides involved female victims, a proportion that has changed very little since 1993 (Catalano et al., 2009). Additionally, over 60 percent of female homicide cases in 2007 were perpetrated by a family member or intimate partner (Catalano et al., 2009).

Like stranger violence, then, violence between intimates occurs at an alarmingly high rate and has the potential to cause serious injury or death to victims. Like stranger violence, too, researchers know much about the characteristics of many offenders and victims of intimate violence. However, compared to stranger violence, much less is understood about the effects of neighborhood characteristics on rates of violence between intimates. This study is designed to help bridge this gap in knowledge.

THE IMPORTANCE OF INTIMATE PARTNER VIOLENCE

Simple assault, aggravated assault, sexual assault, and rape occur between partners in intimate relationships every year (Catalano et al., 2009). Estimates of yearly intimate partner violence (IPV) between couples vary widely – data from the National Survey of Families and Households (NSFH) approximates that three percent of U.S. couples engage in intimate violence each year (Brush, 1990), while data from the National Family Violence Survey (NFVS) estimates that over 16 percent of U.S. couples are involved in IPV each year (Straus, Gelles, & Steinmetz, 2006). Furthermore, survey data from the National Crime Victimization Survey (NCVS) indicates that approximately 11 percent of *all* violence occurs in the family, while an additional 6.3 percent occurs between non-married partners (Durose, Harlow, Langan, Motivans, Rantala, Smith, & Constantin, 2005).

This violence affects victims, offenders, third-party individuals, and children. IPV can cause physical injury and emotional trauma to victims (Benson et al., 2000; Gelles & Straus, 1988; McCann, Sakheim, & Abrahamson, 1988). In many cases, victims of IPV experience anxiety, fear, shame, anger, confusion, and a sense of betrayal, while some may begin to believe that they deserve the violence from their partner. Such feelings can lead to lowered self-concepts, depression, feelings of powerlessness, and post-traumatic stress disorder (DeMaris & Kaukinen, 2005; McCann et al., 1988). Victims of IPV may turn to alcohol or drug use to cope with the emotional and physical scars of partner violence (Kilpatrick, Acierno, Resnick, Saunders, & Best, 1997), or they may recoil from friends and family members (McCann et al., 1988). They may also turn to violence themselves, either by attacking their attacker or lashing out on other, often smaller and weaker members of the family (Gelles & Straus, 1988).

Intimate partner violence within families often disrupts the cohesion, dynamics, and social exchanges that exist between family members (Goode, 1971). Family disruption and conflict, in turn, may lead to future criminal behavior (Sampson & Laub, 1993) committed by the offenders, victims, or children. Additionally, IPV has been found to promote a cycle of violence that occurs between family members and may be used by future generations (White & Widom, 2003; Widom, 1989). It is estimated that over 60 percent of IPV cases are witnessed either directly or indirectly (e.g., hearing violence, seeing the aftermath of violence) by children in the home (Catalano et al., 2009; Clements, Oxtoby, & Ogle, 2008; Holt, Buckley, & Whelan, 2008). Witnessing IPV as a child is linked to problematic internalizing and externalizing behaviors such as post traumatic stress disorder (PTSD), depression, anxiety, delinquency, alcohol problems, drug use, and IPV perpetration as an adult (Holt et al., 2008; White & Widom, 2003). Finally, intimate partner violence can also bring offenders and their families into contact with the criminal justice system (Benson et al., 2000), which may then lead to blocked opportunities for future job placements (Rose & Clear, 1998), and may further disrupt family situations (Anderson, 1999; Rose & Clear, 1998; Wilson, 1987). Clearly, IPV is a problem that affects a significant proportion of individuals and families and that has a multitude of serious consequences for the parties involved.

Individual- and Couple-Level Predictors of Intimate Partner Violence

Because IPV has so many and such far-reaching consequences, researchers have studied its causes and correlates for nearly four decades. Scholars have examined the characteristics of the victims and offenders, the causes and consequences of IPV, and treatment for IPV in an effort to explain, predict, and prevent its occurrence. Historically, research on partner violence has focused primarily on the individual- and couple-level factors which are associated with IPV. Race (e.g., Plass, 1993), age (e.g., DeMaris, Benson, Fox, Hill, & Van Wyk, 2003; Yount, 2005), socioeconomic status (e.g., Lockhart, 1987; Yount, 2005), employment and educational attainment (e.g., MacMillian &

Gartner, 1999), alcohol and drug use (e.g., Kaufman Kantor & Straus, 1987; Caetano et al., 2008), traditional gender ideologies (e.g., Sugarman & Frankel, 1996; Yount & Li, 2009), and access to social support (e.g., Stets, 1991; Yount, 2005) have been identified as consistent individual-level predictors of IPV. Couple-level predictors of IPV include relationship or marital status (e.g., Yllo & Straus, 1981), relationship duration (DeMaris et al., 2003), number of children in the household (DeMaris et al., 2003; Yount, 2005), employment dynamics between partners (e.g., MacMillian & Gartner, 1999), and traditional gender role ideologies (e.g., Sugarman & Frankel, 1996; Yount & Li, 2009).

Specifically, young, minority individuals in low socio-economic strata with low education and employment attainment, who use drugs or abuse alcohol, hold traditional gender role ideologies and who have low support from others are at increased risk to experience or engage in IPV with their partner. Unmarried, cohabiting couples, who have been together for short periods of time, live with and provide for multiple children, and who hold non-egalitarian views on gender roles are more likely to experience IPV than couples without such characteristics. Additionally, couples in which partners hold unequal employment status are also at increased risk for experiencing partner violence.

CONTEXTUAL EFFECTS ON INTIMATE PARTNER VIOLENCE

While race, age, and the other factors mentioned above are obviously important, they do not capture the whole picture. Recent research indicates that neighborhood characteristics also play an important role in the occurrence of IPV. In particular, neighborhood concentrated disadvantage and resource deprivation have been examined regarding their relationship with IPV. Higher levels of IPV have been found in areas that are characterized by disadvantage (Benson et al., 2000; Benson, Fox, DeMaris, & Van Wyk, 2003; Benson, Wooldredge, Thistlethwaite, & Fox, 2004; Browning, 2002; Lauritsen & White, 2001; Van Wyk, Benson, Fox, & DeMaris, 2003; Wright & Benson, 2010) and resource deprivation (Miles-Doan, 1998); empirical research from representative community samples (Benson et al., 2000; Benson et al., 2003; Benson et al., 2004; Browning, 2002; Wright & Benson, 2010), victimization surveys (Lauirtsen & White, 2001; Lauritsen & Schaum, 2004), and police-reported incidents (Miles-Doan, 1998), have established this relationship.

Social disorganization provides a useful theory with which to explain neighborhood variation in IPV rates and potential neighborhood effects on IPV. According to social disorganization theory, several aspects of community characteristics may influence local crime, and similarly, IPV rates. As originally formulated, social disorganization theory held that the structural characteristics of neighborhoods, such as severe economic disadvantage, high residential mobility, and pronounced ethnic heterogeneity, undermined the control capacity of neighborhoods which led to high crime rates (Shaw & McKay, 1942). Empirical evidence has corroborated this theoretical link; neighborhood characteristics such as concentrated disadvantage, residential mobility, and ethnic heterogeneity have been found to maintain direct and indirect effects on neighborhood street crime rates (Bursik & Webb, 1982; Hipp, Tita, & Boggess, 2009; Lowenkamp, Cullen, & Pratt, 2003; Sampson & Groves, 1989; Sampson, Raudenbush, & Earls, 1997; Shaw & McKay, 1942; Steart & Simons, 2010; Veysey & Messner, 1999; Warner & Pierce, 1993; Xie & McDowall, 2008).

Subsequent research has found evidence suggesting that other social mechanisms such as collective efficacy (Maimon & Browning, 2010; Mazerolle, Wickes, & McBroom, 2010; Morenoff, Sampson, & Raudenbush, 2001; Sampson et al., 1997), social ties (Bellair, 1997; Warner & Wilcox Rountree, 1997; Wilcox Rountree & Warner, 1999; Wilkinson, 2007), and cultural norms or cognitive landscapes (Hipp et al., 2009; Sampson & Bartusch, 1998; Sampson & Wilson, 1995) may also act as intervening mechanisms. They partially mediate the effects of disadvantage, residential mobility, and heterogeneity on neighborhood crime rates. These intervening mechanisms are therefore considered more proximate influences on crime rates, and also help to explain variation in crime rates across neighborhoods.

In addition, the unique effects of physical and social disorder, often symbolized by "broken windows," have been examined with regard to street crime (e.g., Wilson & Kelling, 1982; Sampson & Raudenbush, 1999). While some scholars report that disorder is a sign of low control and therefore causally related to crime (Ross & Mirowsky, 2009; Ross, Mirowsky, & Pribesh, 2001; Wilson & Kelling, 1982), others report that the observed relationship between disorder and crime is caused by some other mechanism, such as collective efficacy (Sampson & Raudenbush, 1999). Regardless of the causal direction, physical and social disorder have been suggested as neighborhood characteristics that contribute to variation in crime rates across neighborhoods.

Importantly, and central to this study, there is reason to expect that neighborhood structural characteristics and intervening mechanisms also effect IPV rates. Indeed, research grounded in social disorganization theory assessing neighborhood effects on IPV has found that concentrated poverty (Miles-Doan, 1998), disadvantage (Benson et al., 2000; Benson et al., 2003; Benson et al., 2004; Browning, 2002; Lauritsen, 2001; Lauritsen & White, 2001; Van Wyk et al., 2003; Wright & Benson, 2010), and the percent of female headed households with children (Lauritsen & Schaum, 2004) are associated with higher levels of IPV.

However, largely due to data limitations, previous research (with the exception of Browning, 2002)[1] has not assessed the importance of intervening social mechanisms, such as collective efficacy, social ties and networks, and cultural norms or cognitive landscapes, on IPV rates in neighborhoods. The effects of physical and social disorder on IPV have also been overlooked in past research. Thus, it is not known whether collective efficacy, social ties, cultural norms, or disorder affect IPV rates. In addition, most previous research has used a variety of different estimation techniques to estimate separate individual and neighborhood effects on IPV rates (Lauritsen, 2001), but has not used multi-level modeling, which is the most appropriate statistical technique to use with multi-level data (Raudenbush & Bryk, 2002).

---

[1] Like this study, Browning (2002) used data from the Project on Human Development in Chicago Neighborhoods to examine the effect of collective efficacy on intimate partner violence. However, the study presented here differs from Browning's in that it examines a different measure of IPV, employs hierarchical modeling techniques, and assesses additional neighborhood social mechanisms.

Furthermore, the majority of contextual research assessing IPV has used two datasets – the National Survey of Families and Households (NSFH) and the area-identified National Crime Victimization Survey (NCVS). Whether the results reported so far on neighborhoods and IPV are valid and generalizable therefore remains an open question.

This study attempts to overcome the shortcomings of prior research by employing hierarchical modeling (HLM, Raudenbush & Bryk, 2002) techniques using data from the Project on Human Development in Chicago Neighborhoods (PHDCN) (Earls, Brooks-Gunn, Raudenbush, & Sampson, 2002), to assess the effect of collective efficacy, social ties, cultural norms, and disorder on neighborhood IPV rates. It is hoped that evidence from this study will inform our understating of intimate partner violence, particularly with regard to the effects of neighborhood characteristics on intimate partner violence rates.

CHAPTER TWO

Individual- and Couple-Level Predictors of Intimate Partner Violence

THE MEANING OF INTIMATE PARTNER VIOLENCE

Many difficulties arise when defining and measuring IPV. Most debate in the IPV literature revolves around whether violence between partners should be measured in terms of the *acts* or *consequences* of IPV. Measuring IPV in terms of either the acts (e.g., hitting or shoving) or consequences (e.g., seriousness of injury inflicted) of violence has been shown to yield different results regarding the prevalence of IPV among couples, as well as the gendered nature of IPV (Archer, 2000; Dobash, Dobash, Wilson, & Daly, 1992). Specifically, measurements of IPV focusing primarily on acts of violence often find high levels of both male- and female-perpetrated violence within relationships (Archer, 2000), while definitions of IPV focusing on the consequences of violence find evidence of lower levels of IPV perpetration among females. Furthermore, when IPV is measured as violence which results in injury, males are more likely to be named the perpetrators of the violence and females are more likely to be severely injured (Archer, 2000).

The differences in results arising from the various measurements of IPV prompted Michael Johnson and his colleagues (Johnson, 1995; Johnson & Ferraro, 2000) to suggest that there are two distinct forms of partner violence, referred to as common couple violence and patriarchal (or intimate) terrorism.[2] Common couple violence and patriarchal

---

[2] Common couple and patriarchal terrorism are not the only forms of intimate partner violence which have been theorized to exist. Johnson and Ferraro (2000) suggest that violent resistance and mutual violent control are two additional forms of IPV. However, common couple violence and patriarchal

terrorism are different from each other in terms of the purpose of violence, the frequency at which it occurs, the gendered nature of violence, and the prevalence of it among couples. Common couple violence refers to violence which largely arises from a specific argument, frustration, or stressors which the individuals or the couple experience (Johnson, 1995; Johnson & Ferraro, 2000); it also occurs relatively infrequently between both males and females in a relationship. Moreover, this type of IPV is said to be gender-balanced, in that women initiate the violence in the relationship about as often as men do (Johnson, 1995). Common couple violence is often defined by the acts of IPV, and finds a high prevalence of male- as well as female-perpetrated IPV (Johnson, 1995).

Patriarchal terrorism, on the other hand, refers to more frequent and serious forms of violence, particularly against females within relationships (Johnson, 1995; Johnson & Ferraro, 2000). This type of violence is said to inflict serious physical harm to women, escalate in seriousness and frequency over time, and be initiated almost completely by males (Johnson, 1995; Johnson & Ferraro, 2000). Patriarchal terrorism, unlike common couple violence, is said to arise from a man's desire to control his wife, and may be just one tactic in the male's general pattern of controlling behavior (Johnson & Ferraro, 2000).

Different methodologies are needed to study both types of IPV. Large national studies which select couples from the community are more appropriate for studying common couple violence, whereas patriarchal terrorism requires more focused investigatory techniques. Patriarchal terrorism is more likely to be found in studies of women in shelters, hospitals, and social work or law agencies (Johnson, 1995). Indeed, Johnson (1995) suggests that the two populations are non-overlapping, and that the type of methodologies and samples used to study IPV will impact the nature and type of IPV that is discovered. In other words, studies which draw representative samples of couples

---

terrorism are both conceptually meaningful and distinct, and have enjoyed much attention in the IPV literature; additionally, violent resistance and mutual violent control may be thought of as subtypes of violence within common couple and patriarchal terrorism, respectively. As such, the remainder of this study refers to common couple and patriarchal terrorism only.

from the larger community will find evidence of common couple violence, while studies which draw participants from domestic violence shelters or hospitals are likely to find evidence of patriarchal terrorism (Johnson, 1995). Although evidence, particularly of common couple IPV, does suggest that females engage in partner violence at high rates, there is also much evidence which suggests that females are disproportionately victimized by IPV. In fact, estimates from the NCVS and NVAW Survey clearly demonstrate that women are at greater risk for victimization by intimate partner violence than men (Bachman & Saltzman, 1995; Catalano et al., 2009; Tjaden & Thoennes, 1998). In 2008, females were victimized by intimate partners at a rate of 4.3 per 1,000 females, while males were victimized at a rate of 0.8 victimizations per 1,000 males (Catalano et al., 2009). Bachman and Saltzman (1995) reported that 52 percent of women who were victimized in the previous year by intimate partners sustained injury, and 41 percent required medical care. Similarly, the NVAW Survey reported that approximately 22 percent of women compared to 7 percent of men are victimized by intimate partners at some point in their lifetimes, with 39 percent of women being injured (Tjaden & Thoennes, 1998). When faced with IPV, many more women (44.7 percent) compared to men (19.6 percent) fear they will sustain significant bodily injury or even death from their partner (Tjaden & Thoennes, 2000). Significantly more women sustain injury, receive medical care, are hospitalized, and loose time from work as a result of violent partnerships (Tjaden & Thoennes, 2000). Because various national surveys have found women to be more at risk for IPV victimization (Bachman & Saltzman, 1995; Durose et al., 2005; Tjaden & Thoennes, 1998), IPV is considered a significant social problem by many researchers and practitioners alike (Tjaden & Thoennes, 1998). As such, this study focused only on violence against women in intimate relationships.

Data for this study were taken from the PHDCN, a large-scale research project which drew participants from the neighborhoods of Chicago, and uses the Conflict Tactics Scale (CTS, Straus, 1979) to assess IPV. The CTS is a survey instrument frequently used to measure violence within relationships; it has been criticized for its focus on the acts of violence and a lack of attention to the context and consequences of violence (see Dobash et al., 1992). Consequently, the CTS has often uncovered evidence of high levels of both male and female violence, and is said to primarily measure common couple violence. Therefore, the violence uncovered by the PHDCN most likely reflects common couple violence. However, there is variation in the severity of violent acts captured by the CTS. Straus and his colleagues (e.g., Straus, 1979; Straus, Hamby, Boney-McCoy, & Sugarman, 1996) suggest that there are minor and severe forms of physical violence which occur within relationships. This study examined severe forms of violence within partnerships, but focused on violence against women.

INDIVIDUAL- AND COUPLE-LEVEL PREDICTORS OF IPV

Currently, there is little consensus on a dominant theory of intimate partner violence, although the two main perspectives are generally recognized as the family conflict and feminist perspectives. Briefly, family conflict researchers argue that violence within relationships erupts from common stressors experienced by both partners, or from a specific argument (Archer, 2000; Johnson, 1995). Feminist researchers, on the other hand, cite societal norms, patriarchal values, and male dominance or control over women as instigators of IPV (Dobash & Dobash, 1979).

Regardless of the theoretical framework, generally, race, age, socioeconomic status, employment and educational attainment, alcohol and drug use, traditional gender ideologies, and access to social support have been identified as consistent individual-level predictors of IPV. Couple-level predictors of IPV include relationship or marital status, relationship duration, number of children in the household, employment dynamics between partners, and traditional gender role ideologies. The explanations for why these factors are risk factors for partner violence sometimes appear to be at odds. For instance, family conflict explanations often contend that these factors create or are associated with stress, while feminist perspectives suggest that these risk factors are associated with attempts to dominate or control women. Nonetheless, the consistency of the relationships between these variables and IPV across studies suggests that failure to include measures of these concepts in models predicting partner violence may produce misleading results.

Race

Minorities appear to engage in IPV more often than non-minorities (Benson et al., 2000; Benson et al., 2004; Caetano, Vaeth, & Ramisetty-Mikler, 2008; Holtzworth-Munroe, Smutzler, & Bates, 1997; Lauritsen & White, 2001; Van Wyk et al., 2003). African American and Latino males and females are more likely to report having engaged in or been victimized by IPV than are Caucasian men and women (Caetano et al., 2008; Lauritsen & White, 2001). For instance, Caucasian females were victimized by IPV at a rate of 3.1 per 1,000 in 2005, while African American females were victimized at a rate of 4.6 per 1,000; falling in between, the average annual rate of IPV victimization among Hispanic females is 4.3 per 1,000 (Catalano, 2006).

It has been suggested that subcultural differences, structural limitations, and/or strain may help to explain the relationship between race and IPV. The subculture of violence theory (Wolfgang & Ferracuti, 1967) states that certain cultures are more violent than others; it follows that minority cultures which are generally more violent than Caucasian cultures might also be more violent within intimate relationships. Similarly, the relationship between race and IPV may be due to cultural differences in the meaning of partner violence (Gelles & Straus, 1988; Holtzworth-Munroe, Smutzler, & Bates, 1997).

Structurally, economic marginalization and blocked opportunities may create stress and frustration within individuals as well as between partners (Plass, 1993). African Americans may face limited opportunities for education, employment, and upward mobility due to their position in society (Cloward, 1959), which is often in the lower socioeconomic strata (Anderson, 1999; Wilson, 1987). These limited opportunities may result in low paying jobs or unemployment (Wilson, 1987), economic marginalization (Plass, 1993), and stress or frustration (Merton, 1938). Such characteristics (i.e., unemployment, low education, financial stress) are often linked to higher instances of IPV and may explain the observed relationship between minority status and higher rates of IPV. African American males are economically marginalized (Anderson, 1999) and thus may have a harder time filling the "breadwinning" role within the family (Plass, 1993). It has been suggested that when men are not economically dominant, they attempt to exert control or establish dominance over their female partners by using physical force (e.g., MacMillian & Gartner, 1999); since African American men are more economically marginalized than Caucasian men, racial differences in IPV appear evident.

Minority status may also be a risk factor for IPV because of the "marriageable pool" (see, e.g., Wilson, 1987) or because African Americans perceive the justice system as unjust (Plass, 1993). For various reasons, including violence and incarceration (Rose & Clear, 1998), the ratio of males to females among African Americans is low, creating a small pool of marriageable male partners for female African Americans (Plass, 1993). A high ratio of females to males may create a situation in which African American males devalue the importance of having a single female partner; they may develop negative attitudes towards females and become demanding, controlling, or even violent towards women. Where the number of marriageable men is small, females in abusive relationships may be less likely to leave the relationship (Plass, 1993). Furthermore, Plass (1993) suggests that African Americans' general distrust of the justice system (see Sampson & Bartusch, 1998) makes them less likely to seek help from the police or service shelters in order to leave violent relationships.

Although the effect of race on IPV is fairly robust, the relationship may be confounded with neighborhood disadvantage (Benson et al., 2000; Benson et al., 2004; Lauritsen & White, 2001; Lockhart, 1987; Miles-Doan, 1998; O'Campo, Gielen, Faden, Xue, Kass, & Wang, 1995; Van Wyk et al., 2003) and economic distress (Holtz-worth-Munroe, Smutzler, & Bates, 1997) since minorities are more likely to reside in areas that are economically and socially disadvantaged (Anderson, 1999; Benson et al., 2004; Sampson & Wilson, 1995; Wilson, 1987). For instance, Benson et al. (2004) found that the relationship between race and IPV was significantly weakened once community disadvantage was introduced into the model. Based on this finding, Benson et al. (2004) suggested that the relationship between race and IPV may be confounded with the community context in which IPV occurs. The crux of this study examines how and why neighborhood characteristics, such as disadvantage, may influence partner violence.

Age

Findings from large representative studies indicate that, like other forms of violence, IPV is inversely related to age (Benson et al., 2003; Caetano et al., 2008; DeMaris et al., 2003; Lauritsen & Schaum, 2004; Szinovacz & Egley, 1995). Younger women are more likely to be victimized, and younger men are more likely to be volatile than their older counterparts. Evidence from the NCVS suggests that women aged 19 to 29 are at highest risk of IPV victimization, with 21 percent of women in this age category being victimized by IPV; their risk of IPV victimization is much higher than women in any other older age category (Bachman & Saltzman, 1995). Szinovacz and Egley (1995) found that a female's age predicts both a male's violence against her as well as her injury, so that younger females were more likely to be victimized and injured. DeMaris and his colleagues (2003) reported that younger couples, in part because they had been together for relatively shorter time periods, were more likely to engage in IPV. Other researchers have found that age predicts IPV perpetration and victimization among males as well as females even when the effects of race, SES, employment, drug or alcohol use, stress, social support, attitudes, family size, and relationship status were controlled (Benson et al., 2004; Caetano et al., 2008; Lauritsen & Schaum, 2004).

A lack of maturity or boundaries and the aggressive nature of the young may explain the link between age and IPV. It may be that younger couples lack the skills and experience needed to successfully resolve arguments and reach compromise in conflicts, which may explain why older couples are less likely to engage in IPV (Holtzworth-Munroe, Smutzler, & Bates, 1997). Young couples are also less likely to be married or to have been in a relationship for a long period of time (DeMaris et al., 2003), and may not yet understand each other's boundaries for acceptable behavior. Finally, younger people are generally more violent and aggressive than older people (Hirschi & Gottfredson, 1983), and this may explain why younger couples are more volatile in their relationships than older couples.

Socioeconomic Status, Employment, and Education

A variety of social status-related characteristics appear to be associated with IPV. Indicators of low socioeconomic status such as low social class, low income, poverty, resource deprivation, low educational attainment, and unemployment are positively related to IPV. The relationship between socioeconomic status and IPV can be explained from a family violence perspective in terms of stress, frustration, and poor coping skills, and from a feminist perspective in terms of control or power (Cogner, Elder, Lorenz, Cogner, Simons, Whitbeck, Huck, & Melby, 1990; MacMillian & Gartner, 1999; Voydanoff, 1990; Wilkinson & Hamerschlag, 2005; Yount & Li, 2009). Both viewpoints have garnered some evidence in their favor.

Employment instability and uncertainty, economic strain, and economic deprivation have been linked to individual and family stress (Voydanoff, 1990), marital satisfaction and quality (Cogner et al., 1990), and frustration (Anderson, 1999; Wilson, 1987). Voydanoff (1990) states that there is a minimum level of economic stability that is necessary for family cohesion and stability; families below this level may be more likely to experience IPV. Economic instability or deprivation may be particularly relevant in predicting male violence towards females – Magdol, Moffit, Caspi, and Silva (1998) found that males who grew up in lower socioeconomic households were more likely to use physical violence towards females as adults than males who grew up in higher socioeconomic homes – though employment has been found to predict both male and female perpetration and mutual violence between partners (Caetano et al., 2008). Economic hardship or strain may also affect partners' behavior towards each other, thus affecting their perceptions of marital quality and happiness (Conger et al., 1990); marital dissatisfaction, in turn, has been associated with higher instances of IPV (Stith, Smith, Penn, Ward, & Tritt, 2004).[3] Similarly, unemployment, limited job opportunities, and employment instability are associated with higher levels of stress and frustration (Anderson, 1999; Wilson, 1987), and can create tension between partners which may lead to marital disagreements, increased alcohol or drug use, and violence (DeMaris et al., 2003).

It has been suggested that economic and/or employment problems may threaten a man's feelings of dominance and masculine identity, and he may engage in violence against his partner in order to re-establish his dominance and identity (MacMillian & Gartner, 1999). This viewpoint emerges primarily from the feminist perspective, and holds that men who experience trouble providing economically for their families feel threatened and less powerful, and use violence in order to regain their power (MacMillian & Gartner, 1999). Even couples who are employed may be more likely to experience IPV(e.g., Caetano et al., 2008), especially when their employment statuses are unbalanced (Atkinson, Greenstein, & Lang, 2005; DeMaris et al., 2003; MacMillian & Gartner, 1999). MacMillian and Gartner (1999) suggest that employment is symbolic to the identities, self-esteem, and power structures between couples. They found that the impact of employment status on IPV depends on the employment status of both partners – a female's employment reduced the risk of IPV when the male was also employed, but increased the risk of IPV when the male was unemployed (MacMillian & Gartner, 1999). Similarly, Atkinson et al. (2005) found that a male's employment status and traditional gender ideology interacted to increase the likelihood that he would engage in IPV. Specifically, these researchers reported that those men with fewer economic resources (i.e., employment) than their wives *and* who held non-egalitarian gender ideologies were at increased risk to use IPV. Yount and Li (2009) suggest that the partner with more resources, economic or otherwise, will have more power in the relationship and that this power imbalance is often supported in patriarchal societies.

---

[3] Felson (1992) suggests that marital satisfaction does not directly influence violence within relationships, but that it interacts with other risk factors (such as alcohol use) to increase the likelihood of violence.

Low educational attainment, which may limit job opportunities and is associated with poverty, welfare, and joblessness (Anderson, 1999; Wilson, 1987), has been found to increase the likelihood of IPV (DeMaris et al., 2003). Magdol et al. (1998) found that low IQ, poor reading ability, and early school departure predicted males' violence towards females. They also found that early school dropout and low IQ among females predicted their victimization; interestingly, though, low IQ did not predict females' use of physical violence towards their partners, as it did among males (Magdol et al., 1998). In a follow-up investigation, Lussier, Farrington, and Moffitt (2009) found that having low verbal IQ during childhood significantly and directly impacted male's use of IPV during middle age. It may be that individuals with low education experience more economic stress and frustration (Anderson, 1999), are more prone to resort to violence when verbal discussion fails them (Gottfredson & Hirschi, 1990), or may lack proper negotiation skills (Feldman & Ridley, 2000; Ridley & Feldman, 2003).

Alcohol and Substance Use and Abuse

IPV appears to be linked to other behavioral problems. IPV is more likely to occur when one or both partners have been drinking or doing drugs (Caetano, Shafer, & Cunradi, 2001; Kaufman Kantor & Straus, 1987; Thompson & Kingree, 2006). It has been suggested that substance use releases inhibitions regarding the use of violence against one's partner, or that it is used as an excuse to justify behaviors, such as violence within relationships, that are normally unacceptable (Caetano et al., 2001; Kaufman Kantor & Straus, 1987). Furthermore, substance use may be used as a coping mechanism for stress and frustration, poor relationship quality, or may be the result of partner violence (Kaufman Kantor & Straus, 1987; Kilpatrick et al., 1997).

While IPV is more likely to occur among couples with alcohol problems, males are more likely than females to be drinking when violence is used (Caetano et al., 2001). However, alcohol use is a predictor of both male and female perpetration of IPV, as well as their own victimization (Caetano et al., 2001; DeMaris et al., 2003; Magdol et al., 1998). While alcohol use may not be the immediate cause of IPV

(Kaufman Kantor & Straus, 1987), it does play a role in the infliction of injury as well as the likelihood of reporting IPV to the police (Thompson & Kingree, 2006). Thompson and Kingree (2006) found that females were more likely to be injured as well as to report IPV to the police when their partner was drinking. Additionally, the combination of drinking with certain occupational statuses and attitudes may be particularly detrimental. Kaufman Kantor and Straus (1987) found that men who drank, held blue collar occupations, and approved of violence were over seven times more likely than men employed at white collar jobs and who did not approve of violence or drinking to use violence against their partners.

The directionality of alcohol or substance use and partner violence has been a concern to IPV researchers for some time. That is because alcohol and substance use can act as an instigator of or a coping mechanism for violence in a relationship. Kilpatrick et al. (1997) examined whether violent assault among women predicted their substance abuse or whether females' substance abuse predicted their victimization. They found that females' substance abuse lead to their own violent victimization, but that females' victimization also lead to their substance abuse. Therefore, Kilpatrick et al. (1997) found that substance abuse acted as both an instigator *and* coping mechanism for IPV. Similarly, Magdol et al. (1998) reported that substance abuse among males predicted their physical abuse toward their partners, and it also predicted their own victimization. Thus, it appears that alcohol or drug use do play a role in the occurrence of IPV – they are robust correlates of IPV and continue to be predictive of partner violence even when other predictors such as age, race, and socioeconomic status are included in analyses (Caetano et al., 2008; DeMaris et al., 2003; Stets, 1991).

Gender Role Ideologies and Attitudes toward Women/Violence

IPV appears to have cultural or ideological roots. Patriarchal ideologies, the desire for control, and values which condone violence have been identified as predictors of intimate partner violence. Sugarman and Frankel (1996) defined patriarchal ideology as beliefs that justify and maintain the social organization of male dominance over females, and Hunnicutt (2009) suggests that patriarchy involves prevalent and entrenched systems in society that foster male domination and female subordination. Attitudes condoning or justifying violence against women and attitudes regarding the appropriate roles and behaviors of women may be indicators of patriarchal ideologies. Explanations for the link between ideologies, control, and attitudes and IPV are often grounded in feminist perspectives on partner violence, which contend that partner violence results from an attempt to control women or establish dominance within relationships (Dobash & Dobash, 1979; Dobash et al., 1992). Patriarchal theories expect that broad norms of male dominance foster the acceptance of patriarchal values among men and women in general, making partner violence more readily accepted (Yount & Li, 2009). Another aspect of patriarchal theories contends that IPV is more likely to occur in situations where men feel inferior to their partners, economically (Atkinson et al., 2005; McMillian & Gartner, 1999) or otherwise, and use violence in an attempt to establish control or ownership over their partner (Johnson, 1995) or her body (Wilkinson & Hamerschlag, 2005).

Males and females who believe in traditional gender roles, such that women's primary roles in life revolve around domestic activities while males' primary roles include providing for and protecting the family, are more likely to engage in IPV (Stith et al., 2004; Sugarman & Frankel, 1996; Yount & Li, 2009). The relationship between gender roles and IPV has often been explained in terms of dominance and control within the partnership; when gender roles are not adhered to, or where power imbalances in the relationship exist, males (in particular) may feel threatened (Wilkinson & Hamerschlag, 2005). Males who hold traditional beliefs, but who are in relationships where the female has more power (economically or symbolically), may feel threatened and may attempt to re-establish their dominance within the relationship by using violent means (Dobash & Dobash, 1979; Wilkinson & Hamerschlag, 2005).

While not all violent men hold traditional gender role ideologies, there is nonetheless an association between such beliefs and IPV; furthermore, ideology may be important in discriminating between severe and minor violence (Holtzworth-Monroe, Bates, Smutzler, & Sandin, 1997). Li, Kirby, Sigler, Hwang, LaGory, and Goldenberg

(2010) found that engaging in traditional gender roles predicted IPV among low-income pregnant women. DeMaris et al. (2003) found that males who held traditional ideologies and who were involved in relationships with females who held non-traditional beliefs were more likely to engage in severe violence against their partners, net of other relevant controls. Likewise, Atkinson et al. (2005) reported that males with fewer economic resources than females and who held traditional ideologies were more likely to use IPV than men with fewer economic resources than females but who held egalitarian ideas. Several studies have also demonstrated a link between patriarchal societies in Cambodia (Eng, Li, Mulsow, & Fischer, 2010), Palestine (Dhaher, Mikolajczk, Maxwell, & Kramer, 2010), and Egypt (Yount, 2005; Yount & Li, 2009) and increased violence between partners, presumably due to the broad social norms in these societies which condone violence between partners.

Traditional sex role beliefs held by women is also associated with their likelihood of experiencing IPV (Holtzworth-Monroe, Smutzler, & Sandin, 1997; Sugarman & Frankel, 1996; Yount & Li, 2009). Holtzworth-Monroe and her colleagues (1997) suggest that women holding such beliefs may be less likely to leave relationships once they become violent, or that women may develop traditional sex role ideologies as a result of the violence (e.g., Sugarman & Frankel, 1996). It may also be that women who hold such beliefs are simply more likely to accept abuse or justify it under certain conditions. For instance, Yount and Li (2009) found that women who had experienced IPV were 74 percent more likely to justify instances where violence is warranted. They also reported that one-half of the Egyptian women they surveyed agreed that hitting or beating one's wife was justified for reasons such as disobeying her husband or for violating expected domestic roles such as childrearing. Similarly, Dhaher et al. (2010) reported that Palestinian women felt that wife abuse was justified when a wife insulted her husband, disobeyed her husband, neglected her children, or went out without telling her husband. The relationship between gender role ideologies and increased risk of IPV is fairly robust; at least two meta-analyses have identified traditional sex role ideology as a correlate of male partner abuse (Stith et al., 2004; Sugarman & Frankel, 1996).

Attitudes condoning violence against partners, like gender role ideologies, are positively associated with IPV. The meta-analysis conducted by Stith et al. (2004) found such attitudes to be strongly predictive of partner violence. Likewise, Sugarman and Frankel's (1996) meta-analysis of patriarchal ideologies found that assaultive males reported positive attitudes towards violence against women, and this attitude was a stronger and more consistent predictor of IPV than gender role ideologies. Holtzworth-Monroe and Stuart (1994) identified and suggested three subtypes of male batterers, two of which, dysphoric/borderline and generally violent/antisocial, comprised males who were characterized by using violence with family members as well as nonfamily members and strangers. This may indicate that many males who engage in IPV are also willing to use violence in non-intimate settings, and may be generally more violent than males who do not engage in IPV. Furthermore; attitudes condoning violence against females may be a cross-cultural predictor of IPV; Koenig, Stephenson, Ahmed, Jejeebhoy, & Campbell (2006) found that norms accepting violence against wives were strong predictors of IPV among married couples in India.

Social Support and Social Isolation

The number of friends and family members that a woman has or the quality of those relationships may affect her ability to leave violent situations. Social support, and its antithesis, social isolation, have been suggested as important factors predicting or inhibiting IPV. Stets (1991) defined social isolation as a lack of social integration, ties, or relationships with others. She hypothesized that social isolation may affect the degree of social support and social control in a relationship, where high social isolation may lead to less social support and social control within relationships, which in turn may lead to more aggression. Van Wyk et al. (2003) note that social isolation keeps violence within relationships private, while also increasing women's dependence on their partners. Social isolation may leave women with few resources (both financially and socially) with which to leave their violent partners (MacMillian & Gartner, 1999; Van Wyk et al., 2003).

Alternatively, social support may provide women with more avenues for seeking and finding help when in violent relationships. Van Wyk and her colleagues (2003) characterized social supports as strong reciprocal ties to others, and suggested that the two dimensions of social support are the frequency of contact with others and the level of assistance given to or received from others. It could be that frequent contact with others may expose the violence within relationships, and assistance from others may help women to escape such relationships (Van Wyk et al., 2003). Friends or family members can provide safe alternative living arrangements or financial accommodations for a woman when she attempts to leave the relationship, and they may also give her advice on where to go or what services (advocacy, legal, or otherwise) she may be able to receive (Hadeed & El-Bassel, 2006; Moe, 2007). In line with Stet's (1991) contention that social control may be reduced by social isolation, Van Wyk et al. (2003, pg. 417) propose that the disapproval of friends and family members could "shame abusive men into desisting from their violent behavior."

Research indicates that social support and social isolation are related to IPV. Stets (1991) found that social ties reduced the likelihood of IPV, even negating the relationship between cohabitation and IPV to insignificance. Van Wyk et al. (2003) reported that social support and more contacts with acquaintances reduced the likelihood of IPV. Browning (2002) also found that social support influenced help-seeking behavior among abused women. He concluded that victimized women who reported having more friends were consistently more likely to tell someone about the violence they had experienced than women who reported having fewer friends. Finally, cross-cultural research also suggests that isolation increases the risk of IPV victimization among women in various countries (e.g., Egyptians, Yount, 2005; Latinas, see Denham, Frasier, Hooten, Belton, Newton, Gonzalez et al., 2007).

Relationship Status and Duration

The characteristics discussed above are found at the individual-level because they affect individual partners' behavior, which then increases the likelihood of IPV. However, researchers have found that couple-level factors also influence the occurrence of IPV. Factors such as the length of time the couple has been together, the status of the relationship (e.g., married or dating), and the size of the family or number of children present have consistently been identified as characteristics of couples (not individual partners) that predict IPV. Marital status, cohabitation status, and relationship duration are related to intimate violence. Unmarried cohabiting couples are at greater risk for IPV than cohabiting married couples (Caetano et al., 2008; Stets, 1991; Yllo & Straus, 1981). Some scholars suggest that the association between cohabitation and IPV is a result of characteristics of the relationship, such as lower commitment between the partners (Stets, 1991), while other researchers contend that unmarried cohabitating couples are more likely to be younger and therefore more violent (Holtzworth-Munroe, Smutzler, & Bates, 1997; Magdol et al., 1998). Indeed, cohabiters are younger and more likely than married couples to be minority, depressed, and use alcohol more frequently – all of which are linked to IPV (Stets, 1991). They are also less likely to have been together for a long period of time (DeMaris et al., 2003) and may still be figuring out each other's boundaries (Stets, 1991). Cohabiters may also have fewer social resources at their disposal; fewer social ties to or support from friends and family in the community may increase the likelihood of IPV, since isolated victims have few places to turn to for safety or intervention (Benson et al., 2003; Stets, 1991; Van Wyk et al., 2003; Yllo & Straus, 1981). Finally, unmarried cohabiting couples with less social support and who are more socially isolated may lack the social control necessary to inhibit violence between the partners (DeMaris et al., 2003; Stets, 1991).

Likewise, couples who have been together for longer periods of time are less likely to be violent (Caetano et al., 2008; DeMaris et al., 2003). DeMaris and his colleagues (2003) suggest that couples of short relationship duration are still learning each other's interaction and conflict styles, and may not have learned how to curb their violence within the relationship. Of course, it could also be that violent relationships dissipate sooner than nonviolent relationships.

Family Size and Number of Children

The number of people living in a household, especially the number of dependent children that parents must provide for and take care of, has been linked to increased risk of IPV (DeMaris et al., 2003; Yount, 2005). This relationship has primarily been explained in terms of stressful life events (Wilkinson & Hamerschlag, 2005) and resource dependence (Yount, 2005). Voydanoff (1990) suggests that economic strain within families increases when the number of dependent children outweighs the number of earners in the family, and Yount (2005) contends that women with dependent children and little financial support may be more tolerant of abuse because they have few alternatives and must rely on support from their spouse. DeMaris and his colleagues suggest that conflict over child rearing practices, disciplinary measures, and supervision may add to the parents' stress, which may increase the likelihood of partner violence. In support of this contention, DeMaris et al. (2003) found that the odds of partner violence increased by 28 percent with each additional child.

CHAPTER THREE

Social Disorganization Theory

As originally formulated, social disorganization is an ecological theory which holds that the structural characteristics of neighborhoods, such as economic status, population turnover, and ethnic heterogeneity, influence the control capacities of neighborhoods (Shaw & McKay, 1942). The model maintains that the breakdown of social control results in the neighborhood's inability to realize common values or solve common problems, a state referred to as social disorganization (Kornhauser, 1978). Implicitly, the theory assumes that the effects of low neighborhood economic status, high population mobility, and high ethnic heterogeneity are at least partially mediated by social disorganization. Social disorganization theory is nearly 70 years old, and has been reformulated, refined, and extended throughout the years.

HISTORY AND DEVELOPMENT OF SOCIAL DISORGANIZATION THEORY

Social disorganization theory was originally developed by Shaw and McKay (1942) to explain high rates of juvenile delinquency in Chicago. This theory originated in the 1920s and 1930s at the University of Chicago, and approached crime from a sociological perspective, which differed from the popular individualistic perspectives of the day. Such a change in viewpoint most likely resulted largely from the changing dynamics of American life. During the early 1900s, the conditions of the United States' large cities, such as Chicago, changed dramatically; immigrants flocked to these cities to find industrial jobs, populations grew, slum and ghetto conditions worsened, and racial and ethnic inequalities became apparent (Lilly, Cullen, & Ball, 2002). It was during this time that Robert E. Park and Ernest W. Burgess, researchers at the University of Chicago, began studying the development and growth of urban areas. From their studies, Park and Burgess developed a theory of urban ecology, which postulated that cities grew in a circle formation from the oldest areas out to the newest areas of the city. They identified zones within this circle and noted that the oldest zone was typically the business and industry section, while the next zone was the zone of transition, followed by the residential zone, and finally the commuter zone (Bursik & Grasmick, 1993; Park & Burgess, 1924).

Shaw and McKay (1942) used Park and Burgess' theory of urban ecology to study delinquency in Chicago. They studied over 8,000 juveniles in three different cohorts and tracked where they lived and moved. Shaw and McKay (1942) found that urban neighborhoods characterized by poverty, population turnover, and ethnic heterogeneity consistently had high delinquency rates. Specifically, neighborhoods in the zone of transition had higher delinquency rates than areas outside the zone of transition, regardless of the race or ethnicity of the people living within these areas. This relationship held true over time and through cohorts. Shaw and McKay (1942) therefore concluded that crime was a function of the area and not the type of people living in the area.

To explain the relationship between neighborhood characteristics and high delinquency rates, Shaw and McKay (1942) hypothesized that urban areas characterized by low economic status, population turnover, and ethnic heterogeneity had weak neighborhood control and weak socialization, a state they termed social disorganization. Shaw and McKay (1942) did not explicitly clarify the causal linkages between social disorganization and neighborhood crime rates (Bursik, 1988; Bursik & Grasmick, 1993), but generally implied that social disorganization was created when population change in an area disrupted neighborhood socialization and control processes and created instability in social institutions within the area. Ineffective control and socialization then led to increased delinquency rates in such areas. Shaw and McKay (1942) found indirect support for their theory in that urban neighborhoods with high poverty, transience, social change, and heterogeneity endured higher rates of delinquency than areas which were not characterized by such conditions. Although they were unable to measure the intervening process of social disorganization, they did hypothesize that social disorganization mediated the structural variables' effects on crime rates.

The Systemic Model

Although Shaw and McKay (1942) did not clearly elaborate on the mechanisms by which social disorganization operated, they clearly indicated that social disorganization was characterized by missing or ineffective neighborhood controls and this allowed crime to flourish. Kasarda and Janowitz (1974) recognized the importance of control in Shaw and McKay's theory. They reformulated social disorganization into a 'systemic' model, where they clarified that community control was exercised and activated primarily through social ties or networks that existed between residents. The systemic model conceptualizes the local community as a "complex system of friendship and kinship networks rooted in family life and on-going socialization processes" (Kasarda & Janowitz, 1974, pg. 329); ties and social networks foster a sense of community, which then leads to community behavior such as realizing common values or solving problems (as was postulated by Shaw and McKay). Kasarda and Janowitz (1974) hypothesized that residential stability was the primary structural factor which exerted the most influence on social ties – residents of neighborhoods with high residential mobility were believed to have fewer community attachments, since residential turnover inhibited the formation and breadth of ties (see also Kornhauser, 1978). Kasarda and Janowitz (1974) found that length of residence had a stronger effect on community social bonds than did the competing community variables of population density or heterogeneity, supporting the systemic model. Thus, in Kasarda and Janowitz's (1974) reformulation, social disorganization continued to be a community control model, but it focused on control through community social bonds and postulated that residential mobility was the primary exogenous factor contributing to community disruption.

Further revisions of the original Shaw and McKay model have also been proposed by Kornhauser (1978), Bursik (1988), and Bursik and Grasmick (1993). These scholars appear to agree with the systemic nature of social disorganization, in that population turnover and community ties are the primary mechanisms by which social disorganization operates.[4] Of Shaw and McKay's original exogenous variables which lead to neighborhood breakdown of control and socialization, Kornhauser (1978) and Bursik and Grasmick (1993) argued that economic status maintains an indirect effect on neighborhood disorganization through residential mobility and ethnic heterogeneity, and that residential mobility and heterogeneity influence neighborhood social control through neighborhood social ties.

It is theorized that neighborhoods of low economic status often have high population turnover because residents do not want to stay and will try to move out whenever it is economically possible (Bursik, 1988; Bursik & Grasmick, 1993). Kornhauser (1978) argued that residents are uninterested in making neighborhood conditions better when they reside in neighborhoods in which they hope to leave as soon as possible. Additionally, areas of low economic status are more likely to have higher concentrations of minorities than neighborhoods of higher economic status for primarily two reasons. First, Shaw and McKay (1942) argued that areas of low economic status are the least desirable places to live within the city because of their proximity to industries. Neighborhoods close to industries are typically dirty and noisy due to the nearby factories, and the residential dwellings of these areas are often run down and in need of significant repair (Bursik & Grasmick, 1993). Thus, areas of low socioeconomic status are more likely to attract minorities due to the inexpensive housing and proximity to the industries by which they are often employed (Bursik & Grasmick, 1993; Shaw & McKay, 1942). Secondly, population turnover or rapid social change hinders a neighborhood's ability to keep threatening groups (such as minorities or immigrants) out, resulting in high proportions of minorities or immigrants within these areas (Bursik, 1988; Bursik & Grasmick, 1993).

Social disorganization also holds that residential mobility and ethnic heterogeneity impact community control primarily through neighborhood social ties or networks. Recall that Shaw and McKay's (1942) original model was reformulated as a systemic model (Kasarda

---

[4] The systemic nature of social disorganization will be referred to throughout this text as the systemic social disorganization model, the systemic disorganization model, and the systemic control model.

& Janowitz, 1974) to account for the importance of social ties in community organization. According to this model, neighborhood population turnover impedes the formation of social ties between neighbors, which in turn, reduces the control and supervision capacities of the neighborhood (Bursik & Grasmick, 1993; Kornhauser, 1978). Racial and ethnic heterogeneity also disrupt the formation and extent of social ties (Kornhauser, 1978). Kornhauser (1978) suggested that racial and ethnic heterogeneity hampers effective communication between residents, which further reduces the ability of the neighborhood to expose neighborhood problems and develop solutions. The result of neighborhood low economic status, population turnover, and heterogeneity is social disorganization, an undermining of neighborhood control capacity and the inability of a neighborhood to realize common values or solve problems (Bursik, 1988; Bursik & Grasmick, 1993; Kornhauser, 1978; Shaw & McKay, 1942).

Evidence

Evidence for Shaw and McKay's social disorganization model, as well as for the systemic nature of it, has been generally supportive. For instance, in 1982, Bursik and Webb reanalyzed the Shaw and McKay data and confirmed that population change disrupted neighborhood stability, regardless of the types of people (i.e., race, age, socioeconomic status) who lived in an area. They found that rapid social change in neighborhoods disrupted the stability of neighborhood social institutions and networks, thus reducing the neighborhood control capacities. Similarly, Byrne and Sampson (1986) noted that population change was an important underlying mechanism of social disorganization. They asserted that population turnover increased the number of strangers living in an area, and strangers then reduced the ability of residents to intervene when problems arose in a community. Residents' inability to intercede and activate control gave rise to conditions conducive to crime, such as social disorganization (Byrne & Sampson, 1986).

More recently, neighborhood conditions have been linked to various outcomes including personal (e.g., Hipp et al., 2009) and property crime (e.g., Xie & McDowall, 2008), victimization (Lauritsen,

2001), and other types of outcomes. Lauritsen (2001) found that neighborhood structural factors increased violent personal victimization, and Baumer, Horney, Felson, and Lauritsen (2003) discovered that neighborhood conditions impacted the likelihood of weapons use by robbery offenders. Neighborhood residential turnover also increases the likelihood of property crime in a neighborhood (Xie & McDowall, 2008) and changes in the ethnic composition (or, 'ethnic churning') in or around neighborhoods impacts several types of crime (e.g., robbery) within and between different ethnic groups (Hipp et al., 2009). Further, deleterious neighborhood conditions related to poverty and mobility increase delinquency (e.g., Bernburg & Thorlindsson, 2007), recidivism rates (e.g., Kubrin & Stewart, 2006), and sexual health among residents (Browning & Olinger-Wilbon, 2003).

Regarding the systemic model, Sampson (1988) found that community stability affected community-level friendship ties, attachment, and participation in local social activities – more stable communities enjoyed more ties, community attachment, and participation. He also found that community residential stability affected individual-level friendship ties, attachment to the community, and participation in local activities. Finally, Sampson (1988) reported that community residential stability affected community social ties in both urban and rural neighborhoods, thus lending support to the systemic nature of social control. Other researchers have reported similar results; for instance, Bernburg and Thorlindsson (2007) observed that social ties were weaker in areas with higher levels of community instability.

A major breakthrough for and confirmation of social disorganization came in 1989 when Sampson and Groves directly measured the concept of social disorganization. They used data from the 1982 wave of the British Crime Survey, a self-report survey, and operationalized social disorganization as low organizational participation in local areas, few informal friendship networks, and unsupervised teen peer groups. The measurement of social disorganization in this way directly tapped the processes linked to weak social control. Sampson and Groves (1989) tested the effects of neighborhood socioeconomic status, ethnic heterogeneity, residential mobility, urbanism, and family disruption on each element of social disorganization as well as neighborhood personal property crime rates. Further, Sampson and Groves (1989) examined the effects of the components of social disorganization on neighborhood crime rates. They found that all five structural variables significantly affected neighborhood supervision of peer groups and neighborhood residential stability exerted the most powerful effect on local friendship networks, which was consistent with the systemic model. Sampson and Groves (1989) also reported that the elements of social disorganization mediated the effects of socioeconomic status and residential stability on neighborhood personal violence rates (with the exception of the effect of heterogeneity on robbery) and partially mediated their effects (with the exception of neighborhood socioeconomic status) on burglary, auto theft, and vandalism rates. Thus, social disorganization was a mediator of larger social conditions, as hypothesized by Shaw and McKay (1942).

There has been subsequent support for social disorganization theory, although not all evidence has been unequivocally supportive of Shaw and McKay's (1942) or Sampson and Groves' (1989) findings. Veysey and Messner (1999) replicated Sampson and Groves' (1989) test of social disorganization using structural equation modeling. Using this statistical technique, they found that not all structural variables' effects were mediated by social disorganization. Specifically, the effects of urbanism and family disruption were not fully mediated by social disorganization. In addition, Veysey and Messner (1999) asserted that the indicators of social disorganization did not measure one single underlying dimension of social disorganization, but measured separate social processes instead. They concluded that their analysis only partially supported social disorganization.

Lowenkamp et al. (2003) also replicated Sampson and Groves' (1989) study, using the 1994 British Crime Survey data. They found that more structural variables were related to the friendship networks and organizational participation elements of social disorganization than were reported by Sampson and Groves (1989) with the 1982 British Crime Survey data. Further, they found that the effects of residential stability and family disruption on neighborhood total victimization rates were not fully mediated by social disorganization. Still, Lowenkamp et al.'s (2003) findings, as well as Veysey and Messner's

(1999), were generally supportive of the social disorganization theory, as well as Sampson and Groves' (1989) findings, thus supporting the systemic nature of social disorganization and the intervening role of social disorganization on neighborhood crime rates.

THE LIMITS OF SOCIAL DISORGANIZATION THEORY

Although the research detailed above is generally supportive of social disorganization theory, research conducted in the late 1980s and throughout the 1990s identified several limitations of the theory. In particular, changes over time in the nature of low status/highly heterogeneous neighborhoods prompted reconsideration of their effects on neighborhood control. Additionally, research indicated that the systemic disorganization model operated somewhat conditionally upon certain factors – the effect of neighborhood social ties on neighborhood control was influenced by the type (Pattillo, 1998; Wilcox Rountree & Warner, 1999) and frequency of ties (Bellair, 1997), as well as the types of neighborhoods in which they were developed (Warner & Wilcox Rountree, 1997). Most recently, emerging evidence suggests that immigrant concentration may be an inhibitor of crime instead of a facilitator of crime, as Shaw and McKay (1942) originally anticipated.

Neighborhood Disadvantage

According to Shaw and McKay (1942), neighborhood racial heterogeneity and economic class were highly related because ethnic minorities were more likely to live in disadvantaged neighborhoods since these areas were less expensive to live in and undesirable. The concentration of ethnic diversity in low economic neighborhoods was then thought to hamper communication between residents and inhibit the formation of social ties (Kornhauser, 1978), thus reducing the mechanisms of informal social control within the neighborhood.

Although some of these propositions have been upheld in empirical investigations (e.g., Warner & Wilcox Rountree, 1997), changes in American inner cities and areas of low economic status called some of Shaw and McKay's original hypotheses regarding economic status and ethnic heterogeneity into question. In particular, Wilson (1987) suggested that the social and economic conditions of the lower economic class changed drastically between the 1960s and 1980s, thus changing the characteristics of the poor neighborhoods that Shaw and McKay studied. Wilson (1987) argued that inner city areas are no longer characterized by just poverty – instead, the combination of racial discrimination, the influx of African Americans into urban areas, and the switch from production- to technology-based industries has resulted in the concentration of poor, unemployed African Americans in U.S. cities. The necessity of college education for employment purposes has further limited the availability of legitimate job opportunities for these lower class residents, and their subsequent unemployment has limited their future economic prospects (Wilson, 1987).

Wilson (1987) referred to the conditions of concentrated disadvantage as the concentration of poor, jobless African Americans living in high crime inner-city neighborhoods from which they cannot economically leave. He argued that the effects of living in these disadvantaged neighborhoods are exacerbated by residential *stability* among the poor residents, but residential *mobility* among those middle-class African Americans who can afford to leave. The escape of middle-class African Americans from disadvantaged areas results in social and cultural isolation among the poorest and most deprived residents. This isolation leaves the remaining poor African Americans without ties or exposure to residents who hold mainstream, middle-class values or beliefs. The absence of residents in disadvantaged neighborhoods who embody, display, and reinforce middle-class or mainstream behaviors leaves disadvantaged residents with no role models from whom to learn appropriate behaviors or 'social buffers' to link them culturally with mainstream society (Wilson, 1987). Thus, Wilson (1987) suggested that neighborhoods of concentrated disadvantage are distinctly different than neighborhoods of low economic status or poverty. Further, while these areas, like the cities studied by Shaw and McKay, continue to experience residential mobility, a certain subpopulation (the poorest and most disadvantaged residents) experience residential *stability* because of their inability to move. Wilson (1987) also noted that ethnic *homogeneity*, not heterogeneity, characterizes these areas because primarily African Americans live there.

Evidence

Subsequent research has supported Wilson's (1987) assertions. Warner and Pierce (1993) found that the effect of racial heterogeneity on crime rates in an area was conditional upon the level of poverty in the area – when poverty was low, heterogeneity increased burglary, but when poverty was high, heterogeneity actually decreased burglary. Similarly, the effect of poverty on neighborhood assault and robbery was weakest in neighborhoods with residential stability (Warner & Pierce, 1993). Warner and Pierce (1993) noted that their findings were not congruent with the expectations of social disorganization, since disorganization theory held that poverty, mobility, and heterogeneity should increase neighborhood crime rates by disrupting control. Warner and Pierce (1993) went on to suggest that the urban cities that Shaw and McKay (1942) studied were qualitatively different than the modern U.S. cities. In line with Wilson (1987), they noted that areas of concentrated disadvantage were characterized by residential stability instead of mobility, and racial homogeneity instead of heterogeneity; they suggested that stability may breed frustration, resentment, and isolation, while homogeneity may lead to social isolation.

Krivo and Peterson (1996) also examined the impact of extreme neighborhood disadvantage, as opposed to neighborhood poverty, on property and violent crime rates. They measured disadvantage with poverty, family disruption, male joblessness, and occupational composition, and found that extremely disadvantaged neighborhoods had much higher violent crime rates than highly disadvantaged neighborhoods. They also found that racial differences between Caucasians and African Americans became insignificant once the level of neighborhood disadvantage was controlled. Thus, their research demonstrated the importance of Wilson's (1987) notion of concentrated disadvantage and reaffirmed the contention that urban areas had changed since Shaw and McKay's time.

Research conducted since Krivo and Peterson's (1996) study has primarily used the concept of concentrated disadvantage, instead of

Social Disorganization Theory

poverty or low economic status, as a primary structural variable influencing social disorganization and neighborhood crime rates (see, e.g., Bellair, 2000; Browning, Feinberg, & Dietz, 2004; Browning & Olinger-Wilbon, 2003; Gibson, Sullivan, Jones, & Piquero, 2010; Kubrin & Stewart, 2006; Maimon & Browning, 2010; Morenoff et al., 2001; Sampson & Bartusch, 1998; Sampson et al., 1997; Sampson & Raudenbush, 1999; Silver & Miller, 2004; Stewart & Simons, 2010; Warner, 2003), and most of this research has reported results consistent with theoretical expectations. In addition, many researchers have since replaced ethnic heterogeneity with neighborhood immigrant concentration, given evidence that much racial homogeneity exists in areas of concentrated disadvantage (e.g., Browning et al., 2004; Gibson et al., 2010; Maimon & Browning, 2010; Morenoff et al., 2001; Sampson & Bartusch, 1998; Sampson et al., 1997; Sampson & Raudenbush, 1999; Silver & Miller, 2004; Wright & Benson, 2010).

Neighborhood Social Ties

Kasarda and Janowitz's (1974) 'systemic' model of social disorganization also prompted much empirical investigation throughout the 1990s. Recall that the systemic model holds that residential stability increases community social ties, which in turn, increases community control and helps to reduce community crime rates. Early research examining the systemic model largely confirmed that residential mobility reduced the formation of community social ties (e.g., Sampson, 1988). However, research conducted during the 1990s revealed that the effectiveness of social ties in reducing crime across neighborhoods was conditional upon certain factors (such as the race of the neighborhoods and gender of ties, e.g., Warner & Wilcox Rountree, 1997; Wilcox Rountree & Warner, 1999), and that differences in the quality and frequency of social ties also existed (Bellair, 1997; Browning et al., 2004; Pattillo, 1998).

Evidence

It was largely assumed under the systemic disorganization model that the effect of social ties was constant across all types of neighborhoods (Warner & Wilcox Rountree, 1997); that is, most research assumed that the existence of social ties between neighbors resulted in greater neighborhood informal social control and supervision. However, as Warner and Wilcox Rountree (1997) noted, whether the effects of social ties were constant across all types of neighborhoods had not been examined. In two separate endeavors, Warner and Wilcox Rountree (1997) and Wilcox Rountree and Warner (1999) examined whether the effectiveness of social ties was conditional upon the racial composition of the neighborhood or the demographic characteristics (such as gender) of neighbors. In the first of their investigations, Warner and Wilcox Rountree (1997) confirmed that the effectiveness of neighborhood social ties was conditional upon the racial composition of the neighborhood; they found that social ties in predominately Caucasian neighborhoods were more effective at reducing assault rates than in predominantly minority or mixed neighborhoods. In addition, Warner and Wilcox Rountree (1997) confirmed social disorganization's expectations that neighborhood ethnic heterogeneity decreases the formation and extent of social ties while residential stability increases social ties.

In their second study, Wilcox Rountree and Warner (1999) examined whether the effectiveness of social ties was gendered, in that ties were more or less effective among males or females. They found that neighborhood characteristics and demographic factors such as gender did indeed condition the effectiveness of social ties. Specifically, Wilcox Rountree and Warner (1999) determined that although males and females experience similar levels of social ties, only female social ties reduced neighborhood violent crime. Further, no neighborhood structural characteristics significantly affected male ties, while ethnic heterogeneity decreased and residential stability increased female ties.

The systemic model also appeared to assume that social ties which are developed through frequent contact between neighbors are the most effective type of ties for control purposes (Bellair, 1997). However,

Bellair (1997) suggested that frequent interaction among neighborhood residents may not be the only type of social ties which are effective at increasing neighborhood control, supervision, and intervention. He examined the effects of ten measures of differing levels of social interaction between neighbors across multiple cities, and found that infrequent, not frequent, interaction generated the greatest effect on neighborhood crime rates. In particular, the percentage of residents who got together once a year or more was the most powerful predictor of social interaction on neighborhood burglary, theft, and robbery rates (Bellair, 1997). Bellair (1997) concluded that there is variation in the frequency of social interaction or ties between residents and infrequent ties are most effective for the control capacities of neighborhoods.

Finally, not all social ties are crime-reducing (Pattillo, 1998). Although the systemic model originally assumed that neighborhood social ties are important because they increase supervision and control within neighborhoods, work by Pattillo (1998) and Browning et al. (2004) suggests that some forms of social ties reduce neighborhood crime control capacities. For instance, Pattillo (1998) found that social ties among community residents in a middle-class African American Chicago neighborhood actually reduced the neighborhood's use of formal control because of the residents' overreliance on informal social control. Her research suggested that strong ties may actually decrease neighborhood control when ties exist between law-abiding and law-violating residents. Similarly, Browning et al. (2004) found evidence for a 'negotiated coexistence' model, whereby dense social ties between neighbors reduce the control capacities of the neighborhood through mutual obligations between law-abiding and law-violating residents. Overall, their research indicates that if strong or dense ties exist between crime-violators and law-abiding citizens, social ties may not be effective in controlling crime as originally postulated by Shaw and McKay (1942) and Kasarda and Janowitz (1974).

EXTENDING SOCIAL DISORGANIZATION THEORY

Collective Efficacy

Although social disorganization theory has enjoyed much support over the years, it is clearly not without problems. As discussed throughout this study, Shaw and McKay's (1942) original social disorganization model was reformulated in systemic terms by Kasarda and Janowitz (1974); since then, the mechanisms by which social control operates have been clarified and revised primarily in systemic terms, which assumes that control is activated through neighborhood social ties. However, research indicating potential problems with social ties suggested that neighborhood social control could be achieved in ways not postulated by the systemic disorganization model. For instance, Bellair's (1997) findings revealed that infrequent social ties could also achieve social control, and these ties were actually more effective at reducing neighborhood crime than were more frequent types of interaction between neighbors. Additionally, Pattillo's (1998) research suggested that strong ties between conforming and law-violating residents hampered neighborhood control.

Given such problems with the systemic model, Robert Sampson and his colleagues proposed a new model of social control in which social ties facilitated, but were not required for, neighborhood social control (Sampson, 2006; Sampson et al., 1997). Missing in the systemic disorganization model, according to Sampson, Morenoff, and Earls (1999), was the purposive action (Kubrin & Weitzer, 2003a) of activating ties and mobilizing resources for social control. The model of 'collective efficacy' developed by Sampson et al. (1997) addresses this limitation as well as other limitations of social ties; Sampson et al. (1997) contend that collective efficacy refers to social cohesion among neighborhood residents and is characterized by their willingness to intervene and activate control for the good of the community. That is, collective efficacy combines a cohesive neighborhood social organization with the notion of shared expectations – it is theorized that a cohesive social structure characterized by trust and mutual support between neighbors sharing the same values or orientations creates a context in which residents are more likely to activate social control

Social Disorganization Theory

(Sampson, 2006; Sampson et al., 1997). Indeed, shared expectations are vitally important to the activation of social control because, as Sampson et al. (1997, pg. 919) state, "one is unlikely to intervene in a neighborhood context in which the rules are unclear and people mistrust or fear one another."

Sampson et al. (1997) state that collective efficacy, like social disorganization, varies across neighborhoods and can explain variation in neighborhood crime rates. As an extension of social disorganization,[5] collective efficacy is affected by the structural characteristics involved in social disorganization, and also incorporates a systemic element. For instance, concentrated disadvantage and residential mobility reduce neighborhood collective efficacy, while neighborhood social ties "foster the conditions under which collective efficacy may flourish, but they are not sufficient for the exercise of control" (Sampson, 2006, pg. 153).

Evidence

Although a relatively new concept for investigators, collective efficacy has already enjoyed much empirical support. In their initial formulation and examination of collective efficacy, Sampson et al. (1997) measured collective efficacy with neighborhood residents' responses from a face-to-face interview. They asked respondents ten questions about the likelihood of neighborhood intervention as well as the level of trust and cohesion among neighbors. Sampson et al. (1997) examined the effect of collective efficacy, concentrated disadvantage, immigrant concentration, and residential stability on neighborhood violence, victimization, and homicide rates; they also assessed the effect of each structural variable on neighborhood collective efficacy. They found that concentrated disadvantage and immigrant concentration reduced collective efficacy, while residential stability increased collective efficacy; additionally, all three variables accounted for 70 percent of the variation in collective efficacy across neighborhoods. Regarding neighborhood victimization and perceived violence, collective efficacy

---

[5] Collective efficacy has also been referred to as a theory by itself (e.g., Sampson, 2006).

partially mediated the effects of disadvantage and residential stability on violence, and reduced the effect of immigrant concentration (Sampson et al., 1997). Collective efficacy also partially mediated the effect of concentrated disadvantage on neighborhood homicide. Thus, Sampson et al. (1997) demonstrated considerable support for collective efficacy as a mediator of neighborhood structural characteristics' effects on crime, as well as its direct effect on neighborhood crime rates.

Collective efficacy has also been examined in relation to disorder. While the "Broken Windows" perspective (see Wilson & Kelling, 1982) posits a direct causal relationship between disorder and crime, Sampson and Raudenbush (1999) suggested that disorder, like neighborhood crime, could be explained in terms of a lack of social control; from their perspective, a lack of collective efficacy could explain the observed relationship between disorder and crime. To demonstrate that the association between disorder and neighborhood crime was actually spurious due to collective efficacy, Sampson and Raudenbush (1999) examined the effects of collective efficacy, physical and social disorder, concentrated disadvantage, immigrant concentration, and residential stability on neighborhood crime. They found that collective efficacy mediated the effects of disorder on neighborhood personal violence, burglary, and homicide crime rates, and that areas of high collective efficacy were also areas characterized by lower levels of disorder. Sampson and Raudenbush (1999) concluded that, with the exception of robbery, collective efficacy and concentrated disadvantage were stronger and more proximate influences on neighborhood crime than was disorder.

Morenoff et al. (2001) also found that collective efficacy was consistently associated with neighborhood homicide even after controlling for prior homicide, and collective efficacy reduced the effect of social ties on neighborhood homicide rates. A recent meta-analysis by Pratt and Cullen (2005) revealed that the mean correlation between collective efficacy and neighborhood crime rates was -.30 across studies, lending additional support for the crime-inhibiting effect of neighborhood collective efficacy. In a series of studies, Browning has demonstrated that collective efficacy directly also reduces several negative behaviors and mediates the impact of structural features on these outcomes. Browning (2002) reported that collective efficacy reduced the effect of disadvantage on lethal intimate partner homicide to insignificance and increased the likelihood that victimized women would disclose their abuse to others. Further, Browning and Olinger-Wilbon (2003) found that collective efficacy partially mediated the effect of residential stability on short-term sexual partnerships in Chicago, and Maimon and Browning (2010) revealed that neighborhood collective efficacy reduced the likelihood of violent offending in Chicago neighborhoods by 14 percent. Collective efficacy may be more proximate to individual and neighborhood outcomes than other mediating variables, such as social ties, and has been found to explain up to 30 percent of variation in violent victimization across neighborhoods (e.g., Mazerolle et al., 2010). Furthermore, collective efficacy appears to condition the effect of certain variables. Browning and Olinger-Wilbon (2003) found that it conditioned the effect of social ties on sexual partnering outcomes and reduced the crime-promoting effect of peer socializing on violence (Maimon & Browning, 2010).

Culture

Social disorganization has also been extended regarding the role that culture plays in affecting neighborhood behavior. Shaw and McKay's original model incorporated elements of attenuated culture and cultural transmission in order to explain deviant behavior across cohorts (Kornhauser, 1978). Specifically, Shaw and McKay (1942) suggested that under the conditions of social disorganization, the socialization of neighborhood youths into law-abiding behavior is diminished (Kornhauser, 1978), deviant subcultures form, and are then transmitted to other generations (Shaw & McKay, 1942; Sutherland & Cressey, 1978). Kornhauser (1978, pg. 120) attempted to classify the mechanisms of cultural transmission under a control perspective, asserting that conditions of social disorganization resulted in weak bonds to conventional values, and eventually to the attenuation of cultural values, or "their distortion, their selective disuse, or their withering away." Weak identification with or belief in conventional values then lead to the neighborhood's inability to provide control (see also Warner, 2003). Thus, instead of a deviant culture becoming ingrained in residents and then transmitted throughout generations, Kornhauser (1978) argued that structural conditions of a neighborhood affected cultural values because beliefs in mainstream values were weakened, not because deviant subcultures were formed or ingrained. Little attention was given to the role of culture in social disorganization tradition until Wilson (1987) introduced the concept of social cultural isolation. Social cultural isolation can be explained in terms of a lack of social ties existing between poor, underclass African American residents and middle-class African Americans. Wilson (1987) stated that, in large part, the structural conditions of concentrated disadvantage create social isolation, since non-poor middle-class African Americans leave disadvantaged neighborhoods whenever possible. Social isolation, in turn, deprives residents of opportunities to observe conventional role models and learn mainstream values from them (Sampson & Wilson, 1995). Wilson's (1987) perspective, then, may incorporate elements of cultural attenuation as well as cultural transmission (Warner, 2003). From Kornhauser's (1978) argument, social cultural isolation can lead to the attenuation of mainstream values; that is, because of the lack of ties between poor African Americans and middle-class African Americans, mainstream culture, beliefs, and values are rarely demonstrated or seen by socially isolated residents, and this results in the disuse or withering away of mainstream values (see also Warner, 2003). From the cultural transmission perspective, social cultural isolation can result in the creation of and adherence to an alternative or deviant subculture by residents subjected to conditions of concentrated disadvantage.

However, Sampson and Wilson (1995, pg. 52) argue that social isolation does not mean that "ghetto-specific practices become internalized, take on a life of their own, and therefore continue to influence behavior no matter what the contextual environment," since such characteristics would reflect elements of a subcultural perspective. Instead, they suggest that community conditions shape *cognitive landscapes,* or "ecologically structured norms regarding appropriate standards and expectations of conduct" (Sampson & Wilson, 1995, pg. 50). Thus, in areas of concentrated disadvantage, the conditions of poverty, violence, unemployment, and drug use foster neighborhood cognitive landscapes which are more condoning of crime, violence,

Social Disorganization Theory

drug use, and disorder (Sampson & Wilson, 1995). Sampson and Wilson (1995) state that the neighborhood conditions emphasized in social disorganization theory – poverty, residential instability, and family disruption – create cultural social isolation and structural social disorganization, which then lead to violence. They imply that reducing social isolation and structural inequality would change cognitive landscapes which condone crime and violence.

Evidence

Sampson and Wilson's (1995) argument has received support. Shihadeh and Flynn (1996) examined the effects of African American segregation and social isolation on African American violence, and found that in addition to spatial segregation, social isolation from mainstream values and role models was important to consider when predicting African American violence. They argued that social isolation can limit African Americans' contact with mainstream social institutions, weaken their attachments to the labor force, weaken their political power, and weaken the value of African American communities.

Sampson and Bartusch (1998) also examined neighborhood effects on culture. They contended that residents' beliefs regarding deviance and the justice system are largely affected by conditions of the neighborhoods in which they reside. Much like Sampson and Wilson (1995), Sampson and Bartusch (1998) argued that the neighborhood conditions of disorganization and isolation foster certain cognitive landscapes among residents regarding crime and deviance. In particular, they asserted that neighborhood conditions encouraged tolerant attitudes regarding deviance, cynicism regarding the legal system, and dissatisfaction with police performance. To support their claim, Sampson and Bartusch (1998) examined Latinos', African Americans', and Caucasians' levels of tolerance for deviance, cynicism about the legitimacy of law, and satisfaction with the police. Their findings revealed that neighborhoods of concentrated disadvantage and residential instability were more tolerant of deviance. Sampson and Bartusch (1998) also found that areas of concentrated disadvantage reported more dissatisfaction with police and more cynicism about the legal system than less disadvantaged areas. Thus, Sampson and Bartusch's (1998) study provided support for the contention that cultural values, norms, and beliefs (i.e., cognitive landscapes) are ecologically distributed and influenced by neighborhood conditions.

Anderson's ethnographic study of the Philadelphia inner city was also influential in incorporating culture back into the study of neighborhoods. Throughout his book, Anderson (1999) described the effects of living in areas plagued by poverty, unemployment, welfare dependency, drug use, violence, and crime, on the culture of the inner city. Although he draws from elements of theories such as social learning, culture conflict, and disorganization, the underlying theme of Anderson's (1999) argument is that neighborhood conditions are intimately linked with culture. Anderson speaks to the effects of living in disadvantage on social isolation, community tolerance for deviance, residents' relationships with police, and their beliefs regarding the justice system. He notes that neighborhood poverty, unemployment, drug use, violence, and crime results in community demoralization, frustration, alienation from the police, low trust in the justice system, and a 'street' orientation counter to mainstream society.[6]

Few studies have measured culture directly, but those which have, have examined aspects of culture related to tolerance of deviance, satisfaction with police, legal cynicism, and the code of the street. Silver and Miller (2004) analyzed the predictors of neighborhood informal social control and found that neighborhood attachment and satisfaction with police were significant predictors of informal social control. Furthermore, they noted that neighborhood attachment and satisfaction with police largely mediated the effect of concentrated disadvantage and immigrant concentration on neighborhood informal control. Silver and Miller (2004), then, provided evidence that cultural values and beliefs (measured by police satisfaction) were mediating factors influencing neighborhood social control. Carr, Napolitano, and Keating (2007) also examined Philadelphia youths' attitudes and orientations toward police. They found high levels of legal cynicism and negative orientations toward police, but noted that when asked how

---

[6] At this point, Anderson (1999) primarily draws upon elements of culture conflict (Sellin, 1938), but he notes that the emergence of the street orientation is an adaptation to living in neighborhoods of despair.

to reduce crime in their neighborhood, youth generally suggested crime control strategies which were consistent with mainstream society's beliefs. Carr et al. (2007) stated that their findings could be interpreted from a cultural attenuation perspective instead of a cultural transmission perspective, since the youths' legal cynicism and negative attitudes towards police were not ingrained.

Stewart and Simons (2006) examined Anderson's (1999) 'code of the street' orientation, and also found that neighborhood violence and disadvantage increased the likelihood of residents adopting the street code. They also discovered that adopting the street orientation mediated the effects of neighborhood disadvantage and violence. In a later examination, Stewart and Simons (2010) found that neighborhood-level adoption of the code of the streets strengthened the effect of the code mentality on individuals' likelihood of violence – that is, the effect of one's adoption of the code of the streets on their violence became stronger when the individual lived in a neighborhood which also condoned the code. Finally, although they were unable to directly measure culture, Kubrin and Weitzer (2003b) examined the effect of neighborhood disadvantage and instability on 'cultural retaliatory homicides' in St. Louis. They found that neighborhood disadvantage significantly increased retaliatory homicides, and provided narrative accounts of such homicides from persons living in disadvantaged neighborhoods. These narratives provided a picture of the cultural element of retaliatory homicides, and helped to demonstrate the direct effect of culture on such neighborhood crimes.

Still, there continues to be questions regarding the two mechanisms by which culture operates in contextual research (i.e., subcultural and cultural attenuation approaches). Recognizing this, Warner (2003) attempted to integrate the two approaches by linking them through neighborhood social ties. Under the cultural disorganization or cultural attenuation model (see Kornhauser, 1978), disadvantage and residential mobility limit social ties and lower the extent to which neighbors see evidence or believe that others hold conventional values (due to the lack of social ties and integration between residents). Integrating the cultural transmission perspective, Warner (2003) suggested that social ties can be thought of as one path by which to share and display conventional values. Few social ties, then, may weaken the use, display, and transmission of cultural values. Warner (2003) reported evidence for her integrated model; social ties increased cultural strength, and cultural strength directly affected social control.

In line with Warner (2003), Browning et al. (2004) also combined the systemic and cultural transmission perspectives using social ties. Browning and his colleagues argued for a 'negotiated coexistence' model, whereby social ties increase the willingness of residents to exert social control (i.e., collective efficacy), but simultaneously diminish the effects of collective efficacy because of the mutual obligations which exist between residents. Mutual obligations between residents, therefore, may reduce the likelihood that social control is carried out on certain residents, which then lowers the overall crime-reducing effect of social ties (Browning et al., 2004). Browning et al. (2004) found evidence for their negotiated coexistence model – areas characterized by more social networks and exchanges between neighbors decreased the impact of collective efficacy on neighborhood violence. Wilkinson (2007) also reported findings consistent with the negotiated coexistence model. In her study of residents' intervention of youth violence, Wilkinson (2007) found that disorganized communities had dense ties between residents and residents with strong ties did intervene. However, residents did not always engage in informal social control because of the fear of retaliation or because law-violating individuals were friends or family members of the law-abiding residents. Thus, while ties did increase the capacity for social control, they also decreased the use and effectiveness of it.

Immigration

Social disorganization theory originally expected that high levels of ethnic diversity disrupted the formation and extent of social ties (Kornhauser, 1978) which then reduced the control and supervision capacities of the neighborhood (Bursik & Grasmick, 1993; Kornhauser, 1978). It was believed that ethnic heterogeneity hampered effective communication between residents, thereby reducing the ability of residents to collectively identify neighborhood problems and develop solutions.

However, Sampson (2008) argued that recently the patterning and effect of ethnic and immigrant concentration in neighborhoods has changed. Contemporary research has documented that, contrary to expectations of social disorganization theory, increased immigration has been associated with *reduced* violence and crime (Browning, 2002; Desmond & Kubrin, 2009; Lauritsen, 2001; Lee et al., 2001; Martinez & Lee, 2000; Morenoff et al., 2001; Sampson, 2008; Sampson, Morenoff, & Raudenbush, 2005; Wright & Benson, 2010). Some scholars have suggested that immigration is associated with reduced crime levels because of the strong social ties often found among immigrants as well as their cultural values which are less tolerant of crime and violence than the code of the streets (Chiswick & Miller, 2005; Desmond & Kubrin, 2009; Lee et al., 2001; Martinez et al., 2004; Portes, 1998; Sampson & Bartusch, 1998; Sampson & Bean, 2006). Strong social ties and social networks may characterize immigrants because new immigrants settle where their family or friends have previously settled and this proximity creates social ties and networks (Chiswick & Miller, 2005). As expected by social disorganization theory, strong ties and an anti-crime culture may increase social control in neighborhoods thus reducing overall crime in the area.

Evidence

Research has demonstrated that immigrant enclaves are supported by social ties among residents and that social ties provide community residents with strong emotional support (Wellman & Wortley, 1990) as well as opportunities for employment and integration in the community (Granovetter, 1973). Further, immigrant enclaves may protect immigrants' cultural identities and their bonds to the values and beliefs of their countries of origin. Although originally believed to increase deviance levels because they promoted cultural conflict (see Sellin, 1938), the cultural norms of today's immigrants appear to be less tolerant of deviance than those of previous immigrants (Sampson & Bartusch, 1998). Thus, not only do high levels of immigrants within neighborhoods build community cohesion among residents through their social ties, their cultural backgrounds may also inhibit the acceptance of high levels of crime in their neighborhoods. Contrary to traditional social disorganization theory, then, increases in immigration in neighborhoods may not lead to social disorganization, but may instead stabilize neighborhoods by creating new social and economic institutions (Martinez & Lee, 2000).

To date, the resurgence in research regarding immigration's effect on crime and its role in social disorganization has been predominantly theoretical. Relatively little research has been conducted to directly examine whether the effect of immigration is indeed mediated by social ties and culture, though some evidence indicates that immigration directly reduces negative outcomes. For instance, Laurtisen (2001) found that immigration population significantly reduced violent victimization in central city areas, and Desmond and Kubrin (2009) reported that immigrant concentration was related to lower adolescent violence in neighborhoods. Martinez and his colleagues (Lee et al., 2001; Martinez & Lee, 2000) found that, contrary to social disorganization theory, immigrant concentration is not related to higher homicide rates among minorities, and Sampson and his colleagues (2008; Sampson et al., 2005) asserted that immigrant concentration reduces the likelihood of violence in neighborhoods in Chicago. Finally, Wright and Benson (2010) examined whether the effect of immigrant concentration on intimate partner violence worked through social ties and cultural attitudes as some scholars have suggested. They found that social ties with family members and cultural attitudes not condoning violence in the family reduced the effect of immigration on IPV to insignificance. Their results lend credence to speculation that immigrant concentrations reduce violence in neighborhoods and do so in part because of strong social ties and cultural attitudes against violence.

SUMMARY OF SOCIAL DISORGANIZATION THEORY

Social disorganization theory, as postulated by Shaw and McKay (1942), is a community-level control theory which holds that neighborhoods with low levels of social control experience higher crime rates (Kornhauser, 1978). Social disorganization occurs when a neighborhood community cannot realize common values or solve common problems (such as crime) because the formal and informal social control capacity of the neighborhood is reduced and ineffective (Bursik, 1988; Kornhauser, 1978; Shaw & McKay, 1942).

As originally formulated, social disorganization posited that structural characteristics such as low economic status, residential mobility, and ethnic heterogeneity undermined the control capacity of neighborhoods, leading to high crime rates in areas characterized by these factors (Shaw & McKay, 1942). The disorganization model was reformulated in systemic terms (Kasarda & Janowitz, 1974) in order to recognize the importance that social ties played for social control. It was hypothesized that low neighborhood economic status led to high residential turnover and high ethnic heterogeneity, both of which then reduced the formation of neighborhood social ties (Bursik, 1988; Bursik & Grasmick, 1993; Kornhauser, 1978).

While the disorganization model has received much support (e.g., Sampson & Groves, 1989; Sampson et al., 1997), limitations of the theory necessitated modifications and extensions to Shaw and McKay's (1942) original theory. In particular, the concept of concentrated disadvantage was argued to be more characteristic of poor inner city neighborhoods than poverty or lower economic status alone (Wilson, 1987). The effectiveness of social ties on neighborhood control was also found to be dependent on factors such as the race of the neighborhood (Warner & Wilcox Rountree, 1997), quality (Pattillo, 1998), or frequency of ties (Bellair, 1997). Most recently, the role of immigrant concentration as a contributor to or protector from crime has been raised and is currently being reconsidered (e.g., Sampson, 2008).

Recognizing the limitations of systemic disorganization theory, as well as the value of new research (e.g., Sampson & Wilson, 1995; Wilson, 1987), the model has been extended by researchers. Wilson's (1987) concept of social cultural isolation provided the impetus for culture to be incorporated back into community theory. Likewise, the importance of social ties was reduced with respect to collective efficacy (Sampson et al., 1997), but their role was expanded to provide an avenue by which culture, values, and beliefs are transmitted within communities (Warner, 2003). Collective efficacy, on the other hand, became a direct measure of social control, moved beyond the problems of social ties, and subsumed the 'Broken Windows' perspective (Wilson & Kelling, 1982) under the umbrella of social control (Sampson & Raudenbush, 1999).

The revised disorganization theory continues to be a community-level control theory of crime; currently, concentrated disadvantage, residential stability, and ethnic heterogeneity or immigrant concentration are considered the primary structural mechanisms which impact neighborhood social ties, collective efficacy, and cognitive landscapes. Specifically, collective efficacy (Browning & Olinger-Wilbon, 2003; Maimon & Browning, 2010; Mazerolle et al., 2010; Morenoff et al., 2001; Sampson et al., 1997), social ties (Bellair, 1997; Bernburg & Thorlindsson, 2007; Warner & Wilcox Rountree, 1997; Wilcox Rountree & Warner, 1999; Wilkinson, 2007), and cultural norms or cognitive landscapes (Sampson & Bartusch, 1998; Sampson & Wilson, 1995; Stewart & Simons, 2006; Stewart & Simons, 2010; Wright & Benson, 2010) act as intervening mechanisms which partially mediate the effects of disadvantage, residential mobility, and immigrant population on neighborhood crime rates. These intervening social mechanisms are therefore considered more proximate influences on crime rates, and also help to explain variation in crime rates across neighborhoods.

SOCIAL DISORGANIZATION AND INTIMATE PARTNER VIOLENCE

As demonstrated throughout this chapter, there has been much investigation regarding the effects of social disorganization on neighborhood street crime rates, such as delinquency, burglary, robbery, assault, homicide, violent crime, and property crime (Bursik & Webb, 1982; Hipp et al., 2009; Lauritsen, 2001; Lowenkamp et al., 2003; Mazerolle et al., 2010; Maimon & Browning, 2010; Sampson & Groves, 1989; Sampson et al., 1997; Shaw & McKay, 1942; Veysey & Messner, 1999; Warner & Pierce, 1993). However, relatively little research has been conducted regarding the effect of social disorganization on non-street crimes, such as intimate partner violence (for exceptions, see Benson et al., 2000; Benson et al., 2003; Benson et al., 2004; Browning, 2002; Miles-Doan, 1998; Lauritsen & Schaum, 2004; Lauritsen & White, 2001; Li et al., 2010; Van Wyk et al., 2003; Wright & Benson, 2010), although the causal mechanisms postulated by social disorganization may be applicable in explaining neighborhood variation in such crimes. This section explicates the theoretical applicability of social disorganization theory to the study of IPV.

Structural Characteristics

In much the same way that concentrated disadvantage, residential mobility, and ethnic heterogeneity disrupt the ability of neighborhoods to control street crime, they may also disrupt the ability of neighborhoods to control violence between intimates. Under the social disorganization model, as described above, concentrated disadvantage may affect residential mobility, ethnic heterogeneity or immigrant concentration, and social cultural isolation. In turn, residential mobility and heterogeneity may disrupt the formation or breadth of social ties between neighbors, while social cultural isolation may weaken residents' bonds to mainstream values which disapprove of IPV (Kornhauser, 1978).

Concentrated disadvantaged has been positively linked to increased IPV rates. In one of the first sociological examinations of IPV, Miles-Doan (1998) found that spousal violence was six times higher in areas of concentrated poverty than in other neighborhoods. Benson and his colleagues (Benson et al., 2000; Benson et al., 2003; Van Wyk et al., 2003; Wright & Benson, 2010) also found that concentrated disadvantage was related to increased neighborhood IPV rates; further, they found that disadvantage influenced the relationship between race and IPV (Benson et al., 2000; Benson et al., 2004). Consistent with social disorganization, Browning (2002) found that concentrated disadvantage was significantly related to partner homicide, but its effect was reduced when collective efficacy was introduced into the model. Lauritsen and White (2001) also reported that neighborhood disadvantage was associated with higher risk of victimization by intimates, but the direct relationship between disadvantage and nonstranger victimization risk was relatively weak. Finally, Lauritsen and Schaum (2004) found that an often-used indicator of disadvantage, the percentage of female headed households in an area, maintained the strongest direct effect on community violence against women. Again, however, Lauritsen found that one-fourth of the relationship between community context and violence was accounted for by individual- or family-level predictors (Lauritsen & Schaum, 2004).

While concentrated disadvantage has enjoyed empirical support regarding IPV, residential mobility and ethnic heterogeneity or immigrant concentration have not been widely supported in IPV research, although more attention has been recently given to immigrant concentration. For instance, Browning (2002) reported that neither residential mobility nor immigrant population were significantly associated with lethal or nonlethal IPV, but Wright and Benson (2010) found immigrant concentration to significantly reduce severe IPV among partners. Benson et al. (2003) also stated that neighborhood residential mobility actually decreased the occurrence of IPV; their finding, however, may be consistent with expectations of concentrated disadvantage, where stability is now associated with lower class residents because they cannot leave disadvantaged areas (Wilson, 1987).

Social Ties

According to social disorganization, concentrated disadvantage increases mobility among neighborhood residents and fewer ties are then formed among neighbors. At the individual-level, research on IPV has demonstrated that social ties are important in the prevention of or escape from violent relationships. Specifically, the number of friends that a victimized woman has may affect her ability to leave violent situations for three reasons. First, women with few ties to others outside of their intimate relationship may have very few people to turn to for assistance (emotionally, physically, or financially) in order to leave abusive relationships (Van Wyk et al., 2003) or to help cope with the victimization. For instance, support may increase the likelihood that victimized women seek and receive help from others (Browning, 2002) Friends or family members can provide safe alternative living arrangements or financial accommodations for a woman when she attempts to leave the relationship, and they may also give her advice on where to go or what services (advocacy, legal, or otherwise) she may be able to receive (Hadeed & El-Bassel, 2006; Moe, 2007). Social support from others can also help victimized women better cope with ongoing abuse or better deal with the aftermath of abuse; women who have survived intimate partner violence are often at risk for developing a range of mental health problems, and the support received from others has been shown to reduce or mitigate these outcomes (Coker et al., 2002). Second, few ties or contacts with others outside of the relationship reduces the chance that violence within a relationship will be recognized, thus keeping the abuse private (Van Wyk et al., 2003). Once the violence becomes publically known, friends or family members may intervene to stop the violence. Finally, social support from others may facilitate cultural attitudes regarding the disapproval of violence within a relationship (Stets, 1991; Van Wyk et al., 2003). Van Wyk et al., (2003) suggest that friends can "shame abusive men into desisting from their violent behavior."

Recall that social ties are hypothesized to reduce crime through increased supervision (Bursik & Grasmick, 1993; Bellair, 2000; Byrne & Sampson, 1986), informal control (Bursik & Grasmick, 1993), and the transmission of acceptable behaviors (Warner, 2003). Thus, neighborhood social ties may inhibit IPV through increased surveillance, subsequent social control, and the transmission of attitudes which disapprove of violence between partners. Neighborhood social ties may increase neighborhood levels of informal surveillance (Bellair, 2000), thus increasing the likelihood that violence within relationships will be made publically known. Public knowledge of IPV may increase the likelihood that the incident is reported to police or that formal intervention would be taken. Social ties may also increase the likelihood of informal social control [7] due to the trust and reciprocity that ties foster among neighbors (Putnam, 2000). Borrowing from Warner's (2003) model, neighborhood social ties may also facilitate the transmission of values which disapprove of violence between intimates.

Alternatively, areas characterized by few ties between neighbors may experience higher IPV rates due to lower levels of surveillance, so that instances of IPV go undetected. Fewer ties between neighbors reduce trust and reciprocity (Putnam, 2000), decreasing the likelihood

---

[7] The negotiated coexistence model (Browning et al., 2004) would stipulate that ties to neighbors who condone partner violence may actually inhibit the reporting of intimate partner violence.

that social control would be activated. Finally, areas characterized by fewer social ties may be inadequate at transmitting values that disapprove of IPV (see Sampson & Wilson, 1995; Warner, 2003; Wilson, 1987).

Culture

Since culture has been incorporated back into social disorganization theory as a mechanism that influences neighborhood behavior, it is possible that culture may also influence neighborhood rates of IPV. Concentrated disadvantage is hypothesized to create conditions of social isolation, where ties between poor residents and those holding middle-class or mainstream values are severed or weakened because of residential mobility among the middle-class residents (Wilson, 1987). Social isolation and concentrated disadvantage then create conditions conducive to crime and deviance (Sampson & Wilson, 1995). These neighborhood conditions foster certain norms and beliefs, or cognitive landscapes, among residents (Sampson & Wilson, 1995). With regard to violence, the cognitive landscapes in disadvantaged and socially isolated neighborhoods may be more tolerant of general deviance, may be cynical towards the justice and legal systems, and may be less satisfied with police (Sampson & Bartusch, 1998; Sampson & Wilson, 1995).

At the individual level, attitudes condoning violence against women have been linked to an increased likelihood of IPV (Stith et al., 2004; Sugarman & Frankel, 1996; Yount & Li, 2009). Furthermore, it is theorized that men are more likely to engage in violence against their partner when they feel inferior to their partners, economically (Atkinson et al., 2005; MacMillian & Gartner, 1999) or otherwise.

At the neighborhood level, concentrated disadvantage, social isolation, and cognitive landscapes may also be relevant to neighborhood IPV. In socially isolated areas, mainstream values which disapprove of violence within relationships or violence against women may not be transmitted to or strongly held by residents. Concentrated disadvantage and social isolation, then, may result in cognitive landscapes which tolerate violence generally (Sampson & Bartusch, 1998) and violence against women specifically. Neighborhoods of low

Social Disorganization Theory

socioeconomic status or concentrated disadvantage also provide limited opportunities for upward social mobility for residents, which may facilitate neighborhood-level alienation and demoralization (Anderson, 1999; Merton, 1938). Alienation breeds cynicism and belief that the justice system is unjust (Anderson, 1999; Plass, 1993; Sampson & Bartusch, 1998); the general distrust of the justice system may make it less likely that women in violent relationships will seek help from police or service shelters (Plass, 1993). Thus, cultural attenuation of violence disapproval and cognitive landscapes which are tolerant of violence against women and cynical towards the justice system may impact neighborhood IPV rates (e.g., Wright & Benson, 2010).

Collective Efficacy

Collective efficacy has been found to decrease lethal and nonlethal IPV rates and increase the odds of women disclosing IPV to others (Browning, 2002). Areas characterized by high collective efficacy may have low IPV rates for at least two reasons. First, collective efficacy involves residents' willingness to intervene for the common good of the neighborhood (Sampson et al., 1997). Residents' knowledge of such collective willingness to intervene may deter IPV. Secondly, collective efficacy may increase the likelihood that an IPV victim will confide in a neighbor or seek help (Browning, 2002). Browning's (2002) findings indicate that collective efficacy may lower neighborhood IPV rates, regardless of the level of neighborhood social ties; however, he did not examine the effect of social ties in his study. Sampson and Raudenbush (1999) stated that collective efficacy is perhaps most effective at explaining crimes which occur in public spaces and can be visibly observed. As such, there may be reason to suspect that the effectiveness of collective efficacy may be contingent upon a neighborhood's level of social ties. That is, due to the private nature of IPV, collective efficacy may be less effective in reducing IPV in neighborhoods where social ties are weak and thus surveillance is low. Lower surveillance may reduce the likelihood that IPV becomes publically known. Furthermore, as Browning (2002) points out, the effectiveness of collective efficacy on IPV may be reduced in neighborhoods which condone violence and believe that partner violence is a private matter.

Disorder

The role of disorder in community theory and its impact on neighborhood crime rates is still being explored (Kubrin & Weitzer, 2003a), but it has yet to be examined with regard to neighborhood IPV rates. Disorder has been found to be a predictor of neighborhood robbery and related to collective efficacy (Sampson & Raudenbush, 1999); as such, it may be relevant to neighborhood IPV. Ross and her colleagues (Ross et al., 2001; Ross & Mirowsky, 2009) suggest that disorder fosters mistrust among neighbors, and raises feelings of powerlessness, normlessness, and isolation. Further, Ross and Mirowsky (2009) found that neighborhood disorder was associated with high levels of anxiety and anger among resident. It may be that neighborhood disorder increases mistrust which then exacerbates social isolation among abused women; additionally, neighborhood disorder may increase feelings of anger and powerlessness among residents, which in turn increases the likelihood of violence between partners. Further, disorder may be a result of low social control (Sampson & Raudenbush, 1999), and as such, may be relevant to IPV when collective efficacy is low. In any case, disorder is a neighborhood characteristic which has been linked to neighborhood street crime (Wilson & Kelling, 1982), but has not been examined relative to neighborhood IPV rates.

EXPECTATIONS

Based on the above discussion, several expectations regarding the effect of social disorganization on neighborhood IPV rates may be considered. General expectations are as follows:
- Variation in levels of concentrated disadvantage, residential mobility, and immigrant concentration[8] will be associated with neighborhood IPV rates.

---

[8] Although most literature has demonstrated a positive relationship between heterogeneity and neighborhood crime, emerging research suggests that immigration concentration has an inhibitory effect on crime (e.g., Desmond &

- The effects of structural characteristics on neighborhood IPV rates will be reduced when intervening social mechanisms, such as social ties, cognitive landscapes, and collective efficacy, are introduced.
- Neighborhoods with large social networks or strong social ties between residents will have lower IPV rates.
- Neighborhoods with cognitive landscapes which are tolerant of violence, cynical against the legal and justice systems, or unsatisfied with police will have higher rates of IPV.
- Neighborhoods high in collective efficacy will experience lower levels of IPV.
- Neighborhoods in which physical or social disorder is evident will have higher IPV rates.

Theoretically, there is reason to anticipate that social ties, collective efficacy, and disorder are interrelated. Therefore, expectations regarding their specific effects are as follows:

- Neighborhood social ties will condition the effectiveness of collective efficacy on IPV rates.
- Collective efficacy will mediate the relationship between disorder and IPV.

In addition, there is evidence which suggests that neighborhood characteristics condition the effects of individual- or couple-level predictors on IPV (Benson et al., 2000; Benson et al., 2004; Lauritsen & White, 2001; Van Wyk et al., 2003). Therefore, it might be expected that:

- Relationships between individual- or couple-level predictors and IPV may be conditioned by neighborhood characteristics such as disadvantage, social ties, culture, collective efficacy, or disorder.

Kubrin, 2009; Martinez & Lee, 2000; Martinez et al., 2004; Sampson & Bean, 2006; Sampson et al., 2005; Wright & Benson, 2010). More research is needed to form a consensus on this issue.

This study does not attempt to address all of the above issues; only the direct effects of structural characteristics, social ties, culture, collective efficacy, and disorder on IPV will be examined. By addressing these lines of inquiry, this study integrates the latest advances in social disorganization theory with the study of intimate partner violence. In particular, this study builds on research conducted by Benson and his colleagues (Benson et al., 2000; Benson et al., 2003; Benson et al., 2004; Van Wyk et al., 2003), Lauritsen and her colleagues (Lauritsen & Schaum, 2004; Lauritsen & White, 2001), Browning (2002), and Miles-Doan (1998). While these researchers (with the exception of Browning, 2002) examined neighborhood structural effects (e.g., concentrated disadvantage) on neighborhood IPV rates, they were unable to assess the influence of intervening mechanisms (e.g., social ties, culture) on IPV rates. This study therefore considers the effects of neighborhood concentrated disadvantage, immigrant concentration, residential stability, social ties, collective efficacy, cognitive landscapes, and disorder on neighborhood IPV.

CHAPTER FOUR

A Multi-Level Investigation of Intimate Partner Violence and Neighborhoods

This study assesses the impact of selected neighborhood characteristics, including concentrated disadvantage, immigrant concentration, residential stability, collective efficacy, social ties, cognitive landscapes, and disorder, on severe intimate partner violence against women. Hierarchical statistical modeling was used to estimate the relative individual-, couple-, and neighborhood-level effects on IPV. Specific research questions addressed in this study are:

1) What are the main effects of individual- and couple-level predictors on severe intimate partner violence against women?
2) Controlling for individual- and couple-level effects, what are the effects of the neighborhood structural characteristics of concentrated disadvantage, immigrant concentration, and residential stability on neighborhood IPV rates?
3) Controlling for individual- and couple-level effects, do neighborhood social characteristics such as collective efficacy, social ties, cultural norms, and disorder, affect neighborhood IPV rates; if so, when introduced into the same model, do they mediate the effects of structural characteristics on IPV rates?

This study therefore assesses the direct effects of individual- and couple-level predictors, such as race, age, socioeconomic status, and relationship duration, on severe IPV. It then examines whether neighborhood characteristics significantly influence neighborhood IPV rates after the effects of individual- and couple-level predictors have been controlled.

DATA AND DESIGN

The data for this study were derived from interviews gathered during the first wave of the Project on Human Development in Chicago Neighborhoods (PHDCN) (Earls et al., 2002). The original purpose of the PHDCN was to examine the development of prosocial and antisocial behavior, and to assess the effects of families, schools, and neighborhoods on adolescent development. The project represents an interdisciplinary approach to studying the sociological, biological, and inter-individual factors that influence the onset, development, continuance, and desistance of antisocial behavior over time.[9]

Data were collected from 343 neighborhood clusters (NCs) in Chicago. The NCs were derived from 847 contiguous census tracts in the city of Chicago. The census tracts were grouped by seven categories of racial/ethnic composition (e.g., 75 percent or more African American) and three levels of socioeconomic status (e.g., high, medium, low); based on these groupings, the census tracts were then collapsed into 343 NCs. Each of the NCs comprises about 8,000 residents.[10] From these NCs, data for the PHDCN were collected in four separate components – the Community Survey, the Systematic Social Observation Study, the 1990 Census, and the Longitudinal Cohort Study.

Community Survey

The Community Survey took place from 1994 through 1995, and surveyed a sample of residents from all 343 NCs; residents were asked questions regarding their neighborhood's political and organizational groups, cultural values, social networks, informal and formal social control, and the level of social cohesion between neighbors. The Community Survey segment of the PHDCN followed a three-stage sampling design where city blocks were sampled within each NC,

---

[9] A full description of the development, design, and implementation of the PHDCN can be found on the project's website: http://www.icpsr.umich.edu/PHDCN

[10] "Neighborhood clusters" and "neighborhoods" will be used interchangeably throughout the remainder of this study.

dwelling units were then sampled within blocks, and one adult resident was sampled within each dwelling unit. The final sample size of the Community Survey was 8,682 Chicago residents.

Systematic Social Observation

The Systematic Social Observation component of the PHDCN was conducted in 1995. Data were collected through direct observation; data regarding the physical, social, and economic characteristics of neighborhoods were gathered using videotapes and observer logs. Of the aforementioned 343 NCs, 80 were included in the Systematic Social Observation segment. Researchers drove down each block of the 80 NCs in a vehicle equipped with videotape recorders and recorded neighborhood and street conditions. These videos were later coded for analysis purposes. Researchers also logged information related to land use, street conditions, and physical and social disorder while driving through the NCs. Each block segment on one side of the street was videotaped and observed – these block segments were termed 'block-faces,' and comprised the unit of analysis for the Systematic Social Observation study. Due to coding costs, only a sample of the block-faces within each NC was coded. Therefore, while 80 NCs were sampled from the larger 343 NCs, only a sample of block-faces within each NC was coded (for further details, see Sampson & Raudenbush, 1999 and Raudenbush & Sampson, 1999). In all, 23,816 face-blocks were sampled and coded from the observer logs. However, due to the cost of coding data from the videotapes, fewer face-blocks, a total of 15,141, were coded from the videotapes.

1990 Census Data

To examine neighborhood structural characteristics such as disadvantage, residential mobility, and immigrant concentration, data collected during the 1990 United States Census were abstracted for this study. Recall that each NC was comprised of a number of contiguous census tracts. To provide census information at the NC level, staff at the International Consortium for Political and Social Research (ICPSR) matched census tract information with corresponding neighborhood clusters[11] and calculated census-derived information for each NC. This study used the data created from ICPSR's endeavor. In particular, data regarding population characteristics such as ethnicity and mobility, as well as disadvantage indicators related to poverty and income for each NC were abstracted from the NC-level census data.

Longitudinal Cohort Study

The Longitudinal Cohort Study sampled 6,228 children, adolescents, and young adults from the 80 NCs and followed them over a period of seven years. Three waves of data collection were gathered from these individuals; this study used data gathered during the first wave of the project, which was conducted between 1994 and 1997. Participants of the Longitudinal Cohort Study were grouped into seven cohorts based on their ages; these cohorts ranged from 0 to 18 in increments of three (i.e., 0, 3, 6, 9, and so on). Subjects who were 18 years old at the time of data collection belonged to cohort 18. As mentioned above, the subjects of the PHDCN were children, adolescents, and young adults. However, during the Longitudinal Cohort Study, interviews were also conducted with the primary caregivers of the children. The primary caregiver was considered to be the individual who spent the most time taking care of the subject. The present study used data gathered from the primary caregivers. The primary caregivers of the subjects in cohort 18, however, were not interviewed; instead, the young adult subjects themselves were interviewed. The young adult subjects answered the same questions as the primary caregivers of cohorts 0 through 15. The subjects of cohort 18 were considered to be their own primary caregivers. Individuals in cohort 18 were included in this study, as well as primary caregivers from cohorts 0 through 15. The remainder of this study will therefore refer to these participants as the respondents.

For this study, variables were merged from several separate PHDCN datasets created during wave 1 of the Longitudinal Cohort Study. In particular, data from the Conflict Tactics Scale for Partner

---

[11] The matching process was conducted by researchers at ICPSR in order to ensure the confidentiality of the participants of the PHDCN.

and Spouse, the Demographic File, and the Master File, Employment and Income, Family Environment, Family Mental Health and Legal History, and the Provision of Social Relationships were abstracted for this study. The Conflict Tactics Scale for Partner and Spouse (Straus, 1979) measured the physical and nonphysical aggression of each partner in dating, married, or cohabitating relationships, as well as the reasoning and negotiation skills used in such relationships. The Master File provided some demographic and administrative information on the respondents, while the Demographic File provided more complete demographic, race, and ethnicity information on them. Information regarding respondents' and their partners' recent employment and sources of income was abstracted from the Employment and Income interview. Family dynamics relating to conflict, control, and morality or religious issues were gathered through the Family Environment interview. The Family Mental Health and Legal History interview assessed respondents and their family members for psychiatric disorders and substance use, as well as their involvement with the law. Finally, the Provision of Social Relationships measured respondents' degree of social support from family members or friends. Most of the PHDCN data were gathered via face-to-face interviews with the respondents, although some data were gathered via telephone interviews.

SAMPLE

In order to use HLM (Raudenbush & Bryk, 2002), this study merged data from two separate datasets to estimate individual- and couple-level effects versus neighborhood-level effects on intimate partner violence. The individual- and couple-level data were derived from the Longitudinal Cohort Study, while the neighborhood-level data were derived from the Community Survey, Systematic Social Observation, and Census components of the PHDCN. The neighborhoods, as well as the individuals sampled for participation in the PHDCN, are racially, ethnically, culturally, and socioeconomically diverse, thus maximizing variation on many of the variables of interest for this study.

Level-One Dataset

The individual-level dataset used in this study contained information from Chicago residents surveyed in the Longitudinal Cohort Study. Recall that this component of the PHDCN sampled 6,228 children, adolescents, and young adults. However, because this study examines intimate partner violence against women in relationships, only respondents who were married or cohabiting with their partners at the time of or within the year prior to the Conflict Tactics Scale interview were included. This reduced the eligible number of respondents to a final sample size of 3,235 respondents nested within 80 NCs.

Level-Two Dataset

The neighborhood-level dataset used in this study examined data gathered in the Community Survey, Systematic Social Observation, and 1990 Census components of the PHDCN. Theoretical constructs of interest relating to neighborhood concentrated disadvantage, immigrant concentration, and residential stability were derived from the NC level census data described above, while collective efficacy, social ties, and cognitive landscapes (i.e., tolerance for deviance, satisfaction with police, and legal cynicism) were derived from the Community Survey data. The constructs relating to physical and social disorder were derived from the Systematic Social Observation data.

Information regarding the outcome measure in this study, intimate partner violence, was provided from respondents of the Longitudinal Cohort Study which sampled residents from 80 NCs; as such, all information gathered during the Community Survey, which sampled residents from all original 343 NCs, were not necessary. Instead, only the 80 NCs found in both the Longitudinal Cohort Study (which contain IPV measures) and the Community Survey were retained for this study. The Systematic Social Observation also included the same 80 NCs that were used in the Longitudinal Cohort Study.[12]

---

[12] Due to the cost of coding videotaped data pertaining to social disorder, only 77 NCs contained data on social disorder. Therefore, all analyses of social disorder were based on 77 NCs, not the 80 NCs described above.

MEASURES

Dependent Variables

Table 1 describes the measures used in this study. The outcome variables were intended to tap the prevalence and incidence of severe female IPV victimization. The measures of IPV were derived from questions taken from the Conflict Tactics Scale interview, where respondents were asked how many times during an argument with their partner in the past year their partner had: kicked, bit, or hit them with their fist; hit or tried to hit them with something; beat them up; choked them; threatened them with a knife or a gun; and used a knife or fired a gun. In previous research, the etiology and use of the above types of behaviors have been associated with different factors than those which underlie less severe types of violence in relationships, such as shoving; furthermore, factor analysis confirms that such violent acts are different than minor forms of violence (Gelles, 1991; Johnson, 1995; Straus et al., 1996). As such, the acts of physical aggression mentioned above are considered severe acts of violence (Straus, 1979; Straus et al., 1996).

Response categories to the above questions were None, Once, Twice, 3 – 5 times, 6 – 10 times, 11 – 20 times, and 21 or more times (coded 0, 1, 2, 3, 4, 5, and 6). In accordance with Straus and his colleagues' (Straus, 1979; Straus et al., 1996) suggestions as well as an exploratory data analysis (to be described), prevalence and incidence measures of severe female IPV were created. The *prevalence of IPV* was defined as a dichotomous measure, indicating whether the female in the relationship had ever been victimized by any of the above acts of violence at least one time during the past year. Table 1 demonstrates that approximately ten percent of the sample experienced IPV at least one time during the preceding year. The *incidence of IPV* reflected the number of times the acts of violence occurred. This variable was created by summing an individual's responses to each indicator of severe violence (e.g., 0, 1, 2, 3, 4, 5, and 6). For example, a male who had beaten his partner up twice and choked her once received an incidence score of three. Higher numbers on this variable therefore indicate more frequent severe victimization.

After an exploratory inspection of the data, it was determined that the prevalence and incidence measures of IPV may tap two qualitatively different forms of partner violence. As will be discussed in detail throughout the following chapters, the predictors of the prevalence and incidence of IPV were different, suggesting that the two measures capture different forms of IPV – namely, episodic violence between couples (i.e., prevalence) and more frequent or persistent violence between couples (i.e., incidence). Although this was not initially expected, it certainly is possible, given the heterogeneity that exists among IPV offenders and behaviors. For instance, there is heterogeneity among the types of individuals who engage in violence with their partner (see Holtzworth-Munroe & Stuart, 1994), the types of violence that occurs between intimates (see Johnson, 1995), and even the acts of violence which are used during IPV (Gelles, 1991; Johnson, 1995; Straus et al., 1996).

Based on this, there is reason to believe that heterogeneity may exist within the common couple violence that is examined here. It must be stressed that the decision to examine both measures emerged after an exploratory analysis of the data showed their predictors to differ. While theory does not assert that the prevalence and incidence of IPV are qualitatively different, it does not preclude such a possibility, either.

Independent Variables at Level-One

The individual-level independent variables were selected based on the discussion of relevant predictors of intimate partner violence. In particular, the male perpetrator's age, race, education, employment status, and alcohol and substance abuse were considered key predictors of IPV perpetration against females. *Male age* was an ordinal variable (1 = < 20 years old ..., 6 = 60 years and older), as was *male education* (1 = less than high school ..., 3 = more than high school). As shown in Table 1, males in this study, on average, were between 30 and 39 years

Table 1: Descriptive Statistics[a]

Variable	Mean	Standard Deviation	Minimum	Maximum
Dependent Variables				
Prevalence of IPV	0.10	0.30	0.00	1.00
Incidence of IPV	0.41	1.84	0.00	36.00
Level-One Independent Variables				
Male Age	3.18	0.91	1.00	6.00
Male Education	1.94	0.91	1.00	3.00
Male Hispanic	0.53	0.50	0.00	1.00
Male African American	0.21	0.40	0.00	1.00
Male Unemployment	0.08	0.27	0.00	1.00
Male Substance Use	0.07	0.25	0.00	1.00
Female Substance Use	0.02	0.14	0.00	1.00
Female Social Isolation	-0.01	0.96	-0.90	3.28
Marital Status	0.13	0.34	0.00	1.00
Family Size	5.34	1.82	2.00	14.00
Income	4.46	1.83	1.00	7.00
Non-Democratic Views	0.41	0.49	0.00	1.00
Level-Two Independent Variables				
Concentrated Disadvantage	-0.08	0.77	-1.37	1.71
Concentrated Immigration	0.30	1.05	-1.01	2.96
Residential Stability	-0.26	1.06	-2.09	1.97
Collective Efficacy	-0.01	0.22	-0.46	0.64

Table 1 (Continued): Descriptive Statistics[a]

Variable	Mean	Standard Deviation	Minimum	Maximum
Social Network Interaction	-0.00	0.17	-0.52	0.63
Social Ties	2.52	0.35	1.96	4.02
Tolerance of Deviance	-0.00	0.27	-0.52	0.61
Legal Cynicism	-0.00	0.07	-0.18	0.19
Satisfaction with Police	-0.00	0.25	-0.48	0.54
Physical Disorder	0.00	0.69	-1.78	1.34
Social Disorder[b]	-0.00	0.91	-1.97	1.99

[a]Descriptive Statistics are based on 3,235 individuals within 80 neighborhood clusters
[b]Based on 77 neighborhood clusters

old and most had not graduated from high school. Two separate dichotomous variables, *male Hispanic* and *male African American*, tapped race.[13] Fifty-three percent of the men in this sample were Hispanic, while 21 percent were African American.[14] *Male unemployment*, and *male substance use* were also coded as dichotomous variables (1 = yes, 0 = no), as was *female substance use*. Unemployment denotes that the male was unemployed at the time of the study or had been unemployed during the year prior to the PHDCN study, while substance use indicates that drinking and/or drug use were

---

[13] Caucasian served as the reference category.
[14] At the time of the PHDCN study, Caucasian, African American, and Hispanics each represented about one-third of Chicago's population (Sampson et al., 1997). The over-representation of Hispanics in this sample may result from the decision to examine only respondents who were married or cohabiting with their partners. For instance, it has been suggested that Hispanics are more likely to be married than African Americans (Sampson et al., 2005).

reported to have caused problems with the male's or female's health, family, or job, or resulted in encounters with the police. Relatively few participants reported such problems; eight percent of males were unemployed, while seven percent of men and two percent of women reported substance use problems. Recall that social isolation among women is theorized to increase the likelihood of their IPV victimization (e.g., Stets, 1991; Van Wyk et al., 2003); as such, a factor measuring social isolation among women was created. This variable was derived through principle components factor analysis of five items, and yielded one factor with an eigenvalue above one (eigenvalue = 2.098; alpha = .625). Specifically, *female social isolation* is comprised of variables tapping whether the respondent has one or more friends that they can tell anything to; whether they feel close to some of their friends; whether they have family members who help them find solutions to their problems; whether they have friends who would take time to talk about their problems; and whether they feel alone even when they are with friends (reverse coded). Higher numbers on this variable reflect higher levels of isolation.

Couple-level predictors of IPV considered in this study were marital status, family size, income, and non-democratic decision-making. *Marital status* was a dichotomous variable indicating whether the couple is married and living together (coded as 0) or not married but cohabiting (coded as 1). Thirteen percent of couples in this study were not married but cohabiting. *Family size* reflects the number of biological and non-biological members of the family living in the household. *Income* was an ordinal variable (1 = < $5,000 ..., 7 = > $50,000) denoting the total maximum personal or household income earned in the past year. Most couples reported earning between $20,000 and $29,000 during this time period. Finally, family members were asked whether the male or female in the relationship made most of the household decisions; based on this, a dichotomous variable indicating *non-democratic views* between the partners was created. This variable indicates whether one partner in the relationship makes most of the decisions for the household (coded as 1 = yes, 0 = no). The measure was designed to identify couples in which power was not equally shared between the partners. Table 1 shows that one partner made most of the household decisions in 41 percent of couples participating in the PHDCN. Put another way, power imbalances characterized 41 percent of the couples in this study.

Independent Variables at Level-Two

The neighborhood-level characteristics assessed in this study were concentrated disadvantage, immigrant concentration, residential stability, collective efficacy, neighborhood ties (i.e., social network interaction and social ties), cognitive landscapes (i.e., tolerance for deviance, legal cynicism, and satisfaction with police), physical disorder, and social disorder. Construction of the above variables follow from previous analyses using the PHDCN data to examine neighborhood street crime rates (e.g., Browning, 2002; Browning et al., 2004; Morenoff et al., 2001; Raudenbush & Sampson, 1999; Sampson et al., 1997; Sampson & Raudenbush, 1999); specifically, three-level item response models were used to create all neighborhood measures except for neighborhood concentrated disadvantage, immigrant concentration, residential stability, and social ties. Social ties was aggregated to the neighborhood level, and concentrated disadvantage, immigrant concentration, and residential stability were created via factor analysis of census data. Specific item response models for each of the neighborhood constructs will be described in detail in the Analytic Strategy section of this chapter.

Based on research by Sampson et al. (1997), concentrated disadvantage, immigrant concentration, and residential stability were created through principle components factor analysis of the neighborhood cluster census data. *Concentrated disadvantage* was comprised of the percent of residents in the NC who were below the poverty line, receiving public assistance, African American, unemployed, younger than 18 years old, or living under female headed households. *Concentrated immigration* was comprised of the percent of Latino and foreign-born residents in a neighborhood cluster. *Residential stability* contained the percent of residents who had lived in the same house for five years and the percent of owner-occupied homes in an NC.

A Multi-Level Investigation 73

Also following from Sampson et al. (1997), *collective efficacy* measured the degree of informal social control and social cohesion between neighbors. Collective efficacy was derived from the Community Survey data. To assess informal social control, residents were asked the likelihood that neighbors could be counted on to intervene if:

1) Children were skipping school and hanging out on a street corner;
2) Children were spray painting graffiti on a local building;
3) Children were showing disrespect to an adult;
4) A fight broke out in front of their house; and
5) The fire station closest to their home was threatened with budget cuts.

Responses were given from one to five on a likert-type scale ranging from "very unlikely" to "very likely."[15] Regarding social cohesion and trust between neighbors, residents were asked how strongly they agreed to the following statements:

1) People around here are willing to help their neighbors;
2) This is a close-knit neighborhood;
3) People in this neighborhood can be trusted;
4) People in this neighborhood generally don't get along with each other (reverse coded); and
5) People in this neighborhood do not share the same values (reverse coded).

---

[15] Following from Sampson et al. (1997), "Neither" and "Don't know" categories were combined and coded in the middle category of "neither likely nor unlikely."

Responses were given from one to five on a likert-type scale ranging from "strongly disagree" to "strongly agree"[16] (see also Browning, 2002; Browning et al., 2004; Morenoff et al., 2001). The internal consistency reliability of this scale at the neighborhood cluster-level was 0.847 (for more details regarding item response scale reliabilities across aggregates, see Raudenbush & Sampson, 1999 and Sampson & Raudenbush, 1999).

Two measures assessed the importance of neighborhood social ties and interaction. Neighborhood *social network interaction* was based on Browning et al.'s (2004) work regarding negotiated coexistence, and measured the frequency of interaction and types of exchanges between neighbors. Specifically, during the Community Survey, respondents were asked the frequency at which they and their neighbors:

1) Have parties or other get-togethers where other people in the neighborhood are invited;
2) Visit in each other's homes or on the street;
3) Ask each other advice about personal things such as child rearing or job openings; and
4) Do favors for each other.

Responses were coded one through four as "never," "rarely," "sometimes," and "often." The internal consistency reliability of this scale at the neighborhood cluster-level was 0.734.

To assess the importance of ties with relatives and friends in the neighborhood, a measure of *social ties* was created. This measure was an aggregated measure of residents' average number of friends and family members (both coded from one to five, with 0, 1 – 2, 3 – 5, 6 – 9, and 10 or more as the response categories) who live in the neighborhood (see also Morenoff et al., 2001; Silver & Miller, 2004).

Cognitive landscapes were tapped with three separate measures. Following from Sampson and Bartusch (1998) and Browning et al. (2004), scales for tolerance for deviance, legal cynicism, and police satisfaction were created. *Tolerance for deviance* was a scale

---

[16] Following previous research (e.g., Sampson et al., 1997), "Neither" and "Don't know" categories were combined and coded in the middle category of "neither agree nor disagree."

measuring neighborhood residents' tolerance for drinking, drug use, and fighting among teenagers. Specifically, residents were asked "How wrong is it for teenagers around thirteen years of age to":

1) Smoke cigarettes;
2) Use marijuana;
3) Drink alcohol; and
4) Get into fist fights.

Residents were then asked the same questions regarding teenagers around nineteen years old (neighborhood internal consistency reliability = 0.511). Responses were given from one to five on a likert-type scale ranging from "extremely wrong" to "not wrong at all."

Legal cynicism assessed residents' beliefs about the legitimacy of the law and normative ideology. Residents were asked their level of agreement to the following statements:

1) Laws were made to be broken;
2) It's okay to do anything you want as long as you don't hurt anyone;
3) To make money, there are no right and wrong ways anymore, only easy ways and hard ways;
4) Fighting between friends or within families is nobody else's business; and
5) Nowadays a person has to live pretty much for today and let tomorrow take care of itself.

Responses were given from one to five on a likert-type scale ranging from "strongly disagree" to "strongly agree."[17] The internal consistency reliability of this scale at the neighborhood cluster-level was 0.570.

Satisfaction with police assessed residents' perceptions of the effectiveness and fairness of police response to neighborhood crime.

---

[17] Following from previous research, "Neither" and "Don't know" categories were combined and coded in the middle category of "neither agree nor disagree."

Residents were asked their level of agreement to the following five statements:

1) The police in this neighborhood are responsive to local issues;
2) The police are doing a good job in dealing with problems that really concern people in this neighborhood;
3) The police are not doing a good job in preventing crime in this neighborhood (reverse coded);
4) The police do a good job in responding to people in the neighborhood after they have been victims of crime; and
5) The police are not able to maintain order on the streets and sidewalks in the neighborhood (reverse coded).

Responses were given from one to five on a likert-type scale ranging from "strongly disagree" to "strongly agree."[18] The neighborhood-level internal consistency reliability of this scale was 0.862.

Physical and social disorder were also examined in relation to neighborhood IPV rates. These measures were taken from the Systematic Social Observation component of the PHDCN and follow from previous research conducted by Raudenbush and Sampson (1999) and Sampson and Raudenbush (1999) (neighborhood internal consistency reliability = 0.982). *Physical disorder* was measured by the visible presence or absence (coded 1 and 0, respectively) of:

1) Empty beer bottles;
2) Cigarettes or cigars;
3) Needles or syringes;
4) Condoms;
5) Garbage;
6) Abandoned cars;

---

[18] "Neither" and "Don't know" categories were combined and coded in the middle category of "neither agree nor disagree."

7) Graffiti which was painted over;
8) Tagging graffiti in the street, sidewalk, or gutter;
9) Gang graffiti in the street, sidewalk, or gutter; and
10) Political message graffiti in the street, sidewalk, or gutter.

Social disorder was measured by the visible presence or absence (coded as 1 and 0, respectively) of:

1) Adults loitering or congregating;
2) People drinking alcohol;
3) Peer group or gang indicators;
4) People intoxicated;
5) Adults fighting or hostilely arguing;
6) Prostitutes on the street; and
7) People selling drugs.

The social disorder scale was coded from the videotaped data of the Systematic Social Observation study. Recall that only a sample of face-blocks in a neighborhood was selected to be coded from the videotapes; as such, fewer neighborhoods (77 as opposed to 80) have data on the social disorder scale. The neighborhood-level internal consistency reliability of this scale was 0.833.

ANALYTIC STRATEGY

Hierarchical statistical modeling techniques (Raudenbush & Bryk, 2002) were used to construct indicators of neighborhood characteristics, as well as to estimate the separate and combined effects of individual-, couple-, and neighborhood-level predictors on IPV. In particular, three-level item response models were used to identify the latent variables of collective efficacy, social network interaction, tolerance of deviance, legal cynicism, satisfaction with police, physical disorder, and social disorder. Hierarchical modeling was then used to examine the effects of these constructs on neighborhood IPV after individual- and couple-level effects had been examined.

Measures of neighborhood collective efficacy, social network interaction, tolerance for deviance, satisfaction with police, and legal cynicism were taken from residents' responses to the PHDCN Community Survey, as described in the previous section. The constructs of collective efficacy, social interaction, and cognitive landscapes cannot be directly observed and are therefore considered latent variables (Raudenbush & Bryk, 2002). The construct (e.g., collective efficacy) is instead measured by several indicators; these indicators are residents' responses to survey questions. Following from Sampson et al. (1997) and Browning et al. (2004), item response models used the responses to the Community Survey questions to create the measures of collective efficacy, social network interaction, and cognitive landscapes. Likewise, item response models used the indicators of physical and social disorder collected during the Systematic Social Observation study to create measures of physical and social disorder (see also Raudenbush & Sampson, 1999; Sampson & Raudenbush, 1999). Higher numbers on each level-two variable indicate higher neighborhood levels of each construct (e.g., collective efficacy).

Collective Efficacy, Social Network Interaction, Legal Cynicism, and Satisfaction with Police

Level 1 model

Following from Sampson et al. (1997) and using questions presented in the previous section, collective efficacy, social network interaction, legal cynicism, and satisfaction with police were created using three-level linear item response models. The level-one models adjusted the within-person collective efficacy, social network interaction, legal cynicism, and satisfaction with police scores by item difficulty, missing data, and measurement error. Thus, within each person, Y_{ijk}, the ith response of person j in neighborhood k, depends on the person's latent perception of collective efficacy, social network interaction, legal cynicism, or satisfaction with police plus random error:

A Multi-Level Investigation

$$Y_{ijk} = \pi_{jk} + \sum_{p=1}^{t-1} \alpha_p D_{pijk} + e_{ijk}$$

Where j is a person in neighborhood k; p is a survey question from the Community Survey; i is a response to a survey question; and $t - 1$ represents the number of items measuring collective efficacy, social network interaction, legal cynicism, or satisfaction with police.

Here, D_{pijk}, are dummy variables representing $t - 1$ of the t items that measure collective efficacy, social network interaction, legal cynicism, or satisfaction with police. α_p represents the 'difficulty' of item p represented by D_{pijk}, while π_{jk} is the level of collective efficacy, social network interaction, legal cynicism, or satisfaction with police for person jk. The level of collective efficacy, social network interaction, legal cynicism, and satisfaction with police for person jk was therefore adjusted for the difficulty level of the survey questions tapping each construct to which that person responded.

Level 2 model

The level-two model estimated neighborhood collective efficacy, social network interaction, legal cynicism, and satisfaction with police scores adjusting for the social composition of each neighborhood. In particular, potential biases in perceptions of each construct resulting from characteristics related to gender (1= female, 0 = male), marital status (dichotomous variables for married, separated or divorced, and single), homeownership (1 = yes, 0 = no), ethnicity and race (composed of dichotomous variables for Latino and African American), residential mobility (measured as the number of moves in the past 5 years), years in the neighborhood, age, and a composite measure of socioeconomic status (measured by a factor of education, income, and occupational status) were controlled at level-two of each item response model. Thus, across residents within neighborhoods and controlling for potential respondent bias, the true scores of the latent constructs collective efficacy, social network interaction, legal cynicism, and satisfaction with police vary randomly around the neighborhood mean:

$$\pi_{jk} = \beta_k + \sum_{q=1}^{11} \delta_q \chi_{qjk} + r_{jk}$$

Where β_k is the level of collective efficacy, social network interaction, legal cynicism, or satisfaction with police of neighborhood k; χ_{qjk} is the value of covariate q associated with respondent j in neighborhood k; and δ_q is the partial effect of that covariate on the expected response of resident j in neighborhood k to collective efficacy, social network interaction, legal cynicism, or satisfaction with police items.

Thus, π_{jk} is the level of collective efficacy for person j in neighborhood k. β_k is the neighborhood level of collective efficacy, social network interaction, legal cynicism, or satisfaction with police after adjusting for the social composition of the respondents in neighborhood k.

Level 3 model

Finally, the level-three model allowed each neighborhood's mean collective efficacy, social network interaction, legal cynicism, or satisfaction with police to vary randomly around a grand mean:

$$\beta_k = \gamma + u_k$$

So that γ is the grand mean of collective efficacy, social network interaction, legal cynicism, or satisfaction with police, and u_k is a normally distributed random effect associated with neighborhood k.

A Multi-Level Investigation

The empirical Bayes residual from the level-three model constitutes the neighborhood level of collective efficacy, social network interaction, legal cynicism, and satisfaction with police after controlling for item difficulty and neighborhood social composition; the empirical Bayes residual was therefore used as the 'true' neighborhood score on collective efficacy, social network interaction, legal cynicism, and satisfaction with police.

Tolerance for Deviance

Level 1 model

Borrowing from Raudenbush and Sampson (1999), tolerance for deviance was created using a three-level Bernoulli item response model. Due to the skew in the response categories of tolerance for deviance, the measure was dichotomized; categories of "not wrong at all" and "a little wrong" were combined and coded as 1, whereas "wrong," "very wrong," and "extremely wrong" were combined and coded as 0. As such, the measure of tolerance for deviance for the item response model indicates whether the respondent was tolerant of deviance or not tolerant of deviance. The level-one model of the item response model adjusted the within-person tolerance for deviance by item difficulty, missing data, and measurement error. Here, Y_{ijk}, is person j of neighborhood k's response to item i of the tolerance for deviance questions coded as 1 if the response is affirmative (tolerant) and coded as 0 if the response to question i of tolerance for deviance is not affirmative (not tolerant). μ_{ijk} is the probability that $Y_{ijk}=1$. The Bernoulli model holds that $Y_{ijk} = \log\left(\dfrac{\mu_{ijk}}{1-\mu_{ijk}}\right)$ so that:

$$logit(Y_{ijk}) = \pi_{jk} + \sum_{p=1}^{t-1}\alpha_p X_{pijk}$$

Where j is a person within neighborhood k; i is a response to a survey question from the Community

Survey; $logit(Y_{ijk})$ is the log-odds of the probability that $Y_{ijk} = 1$; π_{jk} is the adjusted log-odds of respondent j of neighborhood k being tolerant of any of the deviance items; α_p is the difficulty of item p within the tolerance for deviance scale; and X_{pijk}, $p = 1..., t - 1$ are dummy variables representing $t - 1$ of the t items that measure tolerance for deviance.

Thus, the probability, $logit(Y_{ijk})$, of respondent j of neighborhood k being tolerant of deviance, $Y_{ijk} = 1$, depends on his or her tolerance of other p deviance items as well as the severity, α_p, of item p on the t-item tolerance for deviance scale. Each X is centered around its grand mean, and one item of the tolerance for deviance scale ($t - 1$) is not represented by a dummy variable in order to serve as the reference item.

Level 2 model

The level-two model estimated neighborhood tolerance for deviance scores adjusting for the social composition of each neighborhood. In particular, potential biases in tolerance for deviance resulting from characteristics related to gender (1= female, 0 = male), marital status (dichotomous variables for married, separated or divorced, and single), homeownership (1 = yes, 0 = no), ethnicity and race (composed of dichotomous variables for Latino and African American), residential mobility (measured as the number of moves in the past 5 years), years in the neighborhood, age, and a composite measure of socioeconomic status (measured by a factor of education, income, and occupation) were controlled at level-two of the item response model. Therefore, across residents within neighborhoods and controlling for potential respondent bias, the true scores of the latent construct tolerance for deviance vary randomly around the neighborhood mean:

$$\pi_{jk} = \beta_k + \sum_{q=1}^{11} \delta_q \chi_{qjk} + u_{jk}$$

Where χ_{qjk} is the value of covariate q associated with respondent j in neighborhood k; and δ_q is the partial effect of that covariate on the expected response of resident j in neighborhood k to tolerance for deviance items.

Thus, π_{jk} is the level of tolerance for deviance for person j of neighborhood k. β_k is the neighborhood level of tolerance for deviance, adjusting for the social composition of the respondents in neighborhood k. The random effects are assumed to be bivariate normally distributed.

Level 3 model

Finally, the level-three model allowed each neighborhood's level of tolerance for deviance to vary randomly around a grand mean:

$$\beta_k = \gamma + u_k$$

So that γ is the grand mean tolerance for deviance and u_k is a bivariate normally distributed random effect associated with neighborhood k.

Again, the empirical Bayes residual from the level-three model constitutes the neighborhood level of tolerance for deviance after controlling for item difficulty and neighborhood social composition; the empirical Bayes residual was therefore used as the 'true' neighborhood score on tolerance for deviance.

Physical and Social Disorder

Level 1 model

Following from Raudenbush and Sampson (1999), physical and social disorder were created using three-level Bernoulli item response models. The level-one model adjusted the within-face-block disorder by the item difficulty, as well as missing data and measurement error. Here, Y_{ijk} is an indicator coded as 1 if indicator i of disorder is present in face-block j of neighborhood k, with Y_{ijk} coded as 0 if indicator i of disorder is not present in the face-block or is missing from the dataset. μ_{ijk} is the probability that $Y_{ijk}=1$. The Bernoulli model holds that

$$Y_{ijk} = \log\left(\frac{\mu_{ijk}}{1-\mu_{ijk}}\right)$$ so that:

$$logit(Y_{ijk}) = \pi_{jk} + \sum_{p=1}^{t-1}\alpha_p X_{pijk}$$

Where j is a face-block in neighborhood k; i is an indicator of physical or social disorder; $logit(Y_{ijk})$ is the log-odds of the probability that $Y_{ijk}=1$; π_{jk} is the adjusted log-odds of finding physical or social disorder on a "typical item" when observing face-block j of neighborhood k; α_p is the difficulty of item p within the disorder scale; and $X_{pijk}, p = 1..., t-1$ are dummy variables representing $t - 1$ of the t items that measure physical or social disorder.

Thus, the probability, $logit(Y_{ijk})$, of finding an indicator of physical or social disorder, $Y_{ijk} = 1$, in face-block j of neighborhood k depends on the presence of other p indicators of disorder as well as the severity,

α_p, of item p on the t-item disorder scale. Each X is centered around its grand mean, and one item of each disorder scale is not represented by a dummy variable ($t - 1$) in order to serve as the reference item. This item is perceived as the "typical item" of physical or social disorder, and therefore has a difficulty level of zero. The model allows that face-block disorder, π_{jk}, is adjusted for missing data. Missing data arise because of the decision to code a subsample of face-blocks from the videotaped data in the Systematic Social Observation study.

Level 2 model

The level-two model accounted for variation in physical or social disorder between face-blocks within neighborhoods; this disorder is predicted by the overall neighborhood level of disorder and the time of day in which the face-block was observed. Five time-of-day dummy variables were included in this model. The times of the day represented by these indicators are: 7:00 to 8:59 am, 9:00 to 10:59 am, 11:00 am to 12:59 pm, 1:00 to 2:59 pm, and 3:00 to 4:59 pm, while the omitted time of day indicator is from 5:00 to 6:59 pm. The level-two model is as follows:

$$\pi_{jk} = \beta_k + \sum_{q=1}^{5} \theta_{qk}(Time)_{qjk} + u_{jk}$$

Where $(Time)_{qjk}$ for $q = 1\ldots,5$ are five time-of-day indicators for each face block j of neighborhood k; θ_{qk} is a regression coefficient capturing the time-of-day effects on observing physical or social disorder within neighborhood k (these are held constant across all neighborhoods).

Therefore, β_k is the neighborhood k level of physical or social disorder, adjusting for time of day. The random effects are assumed to be bivariate normally distributed.

Level 3 model

Finally, the level-three model allowed each neighborhood's level of physical or social disorder to vary randomly around a grand mean:

$\beta_k = \gamma + u_k$

So that γ is the grand mean physical or social disorder and u_k is a bivariate normally distributed random effect associated with neighborhood k.

Again, the empirical Bayes residual from the level-three model constitutes the neighborhood level of disorder after controlling for item difficulty and time-of-day effects; the empirical Bayes residual was therefore used as the 'true' neighborhood score on physical or social disorder.

Analytic Procedures

HLM 6 (Raudenbush, Bryk, Cheong, Congdon, & du Toit, 2004) was used to estimate the effects of individual- and couple-level (level-one) as well as neighborhood-level (level-two) predictors on intimate partner violence. The prevalence of severe female IPV victimization was examined using a Bernoulli model, and the incidence of IPV was examined with a Negative Binomial model, which takes into account over-dispersed (i.e., large variance) and skewed outcome measures (Raudenbush & Bryk, 2002).

For each IPV measure (i.e., prevalence and incidence), HLM examines different outcomes at level-one and level-two. Specifically, when examining the prevalence of IPV, the level-one outcome in the hierarchical Bernoulli model is the log-odds of an individual experiencing IPV at least one time during the past year, whereas the outcome at level-two is the proportion of individuals within each NC experiencing IPV in the past year. Likewise, for the incidence of IPV, the level-one outcome is the number of times a man engaged in IPV against his partner, while the outcome at level-two is the average number of times IPV occurs within a neighborhood cluster (this is an average of all violent and nonviolent couples in a neighborhood). Thus, both level-two outcomes examined in hierarchical models are rates; for the remainder of this study, the level-two prevalence and incidence outcomes will be referred to as the prevalence rate and incidence rate, respectively.

Due to the different outcomes used in multi-level modeling, multiple steps were necessary in order to determine whether each outcome significantly varied across individuals as well as aggregates. The first step for each bi-level model involved deriving estimates of variance in each outcome for each level of analysis – that is, determining the variance existing in the outcome at level-one as well as at level-two. This involved determining whether the variance between neighborhoods was significant ($p \leq .05$); this is necessary in order to justify the examination of neighborhood IPV rates – if the rates of IPV victimization did not significantly vary between neighborhoods, there would be no reason to model the level-two effects (such as neighborhood characteristics) on the level-two outcomes (such as rates of severe neighborhood IPV).

The second step, examining "random coefficients" models, involved the estimation of individual- and couple-level (level-one) predictors on each IPV outcome. This allowed for the examination of the significance and magnitude of those effects, as well as a determination of which effects differ significantly across neighborhoods (at the $p < .05$ level). The random coefficients model determines whether certain level-one relationships with IPV, such as marital status, vary significantly across neighborhoods. For the prevalence of IPV, the effects of males' education level and race (Hispanic and African American) did not vary significantly across neighborhood clusters, and were therefore "fixed" for the estimation of all subsequent models (e.g., "intercepts-as-outcomes," described next). For the incidence of IPV, the effects of male education, race (Hispanic and African American), substance use, female substance use, and marital status did not significantly vary across neighborhoods, and were also "fixed" for all subsequent analyses. All level-one predictors were grand mean-centered in order to determine the proportions of between-neighborhood variance in IPV outcomes which are explained by the compositional differences of neighborhoods.

The third step, the "intercepts-as-outcome" models, examined the main effects of neighborhood characteristics (e.g., collective efficacy) on the outcomes at level-two (e.g., neighborhood rates of severe female IPV victimization, the mean number of IPV victimizations per neighborhood). This step also allowed all fixed and varying level-one predictors to influence the outcome before the effects of neighborhood variables were estimated. Thus, this model allowed for the estimation of neighborhood effects on neighborhood IPV outcomes after level-one predictors had been controlled. The results of these analyses are provided in Tables 2 through 21.

Benefits of Hierarchical Modeling Techniques

It is important to note the benefits of hierarchical modeling (Raudenbush & Bryk, 2002) for multi-level data such as those used in this study. Pooled regression techniques, which include variables based on two separate units of analysis (e.g., individual and aggregate) in the same model, may be biased modeling techniques to use with multi-level data. Raudenbush and Bryk (2002) contend that correlated error, heteroskedasticity, and biased hypothesis tests may produce inaccurate results when using pooled regression analyses. Specifically, correlated error exists among individuals within aggregates because the individuals are not randomly distributed across the aggregates, while heteroskedasticity exists at the aggregate level because of unequal numbers of individuals existing within each aggregate. Also, tests of null hypotheses at the aggregate level are based on the wrong unit of analysis; that is, they are based on the number of *individuals* within the sample instead of the number of *aggregates* within the sample, which is the appropriate unit of analysis to examine (Raudenbush & Bryk, 2002). These problems may create misleading results when examining individual- and aggregate-level data with pooled regression techniques.

Hierarchical linear modeling (HLM, Raudenbush & Bryk, 2002) is designed to address such problems, and has been found to provide more reliable hypothesis tests, valid parameter estimates, and consistency in estimates across both levels of analysis (Wooldredge, Griffin, & Pratt, 2001). Specifically, HLM nests level-one units (i.e., individuals) within level-two units (i.e., neighborhood clusters); this recognizes that individuals are not independent of the aggregates, and adjusts for the problems created by correlated error. HLM also uses generalized least squares techniques to address the heteroskedasticity that results from unequal numbers of individuals existing within aggregates (Raudenbush & Bryk, 2002). Finally, HLM bases hypotheses tests at the aggregate level on the number aggregates in the sample instead of the total number of individuals in the sample; this provides for more reliable hypothesis tests. For these reasons, hierarchical modeling has become the technique of choice to use with multi-level data in criminological and sociological research. As mentioned previously, data limitations have precluded previous researchers from using hierarchical modeling techniques to examine the neighborhood effects on partner violence. This study attempts to address this limitation.

CHAPTER FIVE

Neighborhood Influences on Intimate Partner Violence

The specific research questions of this study involved assessing: 1) the main effects of individual- and couple-level characteristics on severe partner violence against women; 2) the main effects of the structural neighborhood characteristics of concentrated disadvantage, immigrant concentration, and residential stability on neighborhood prevalence and incidence rates of IPV, controlling for individual- and couple-level effects; 3) the main effects of the social and cultural mechanisms of neighborhood collective efficacy, ties, cultural norms, and disorder on neighborhood IPV rates, controlling for individual- and couple-level effects; and finally, 4) whether these characteristics mediate the relationships between neighborhood structural characteristics and IPV. Results of this study are presented in Tables 2 through 21. For each IPV measure, the level-one random coefficients model, which examines the individual- and couple-level effects on IPV are first examined, and the hierarchical models assessing the neighborhood effects on IPV are then presented.

PREVALENCE OF INTIMATE PARTNER VIOLENCE

Level-One Random Coefficients Model

The following sections utilized hierarchical Bernoulli models to assess the predictors of the prevalence of IPV. Table 2 depicts the findings from the random coefficients Bernoulli model, which estimated the individual- and couple-level (level-one) effects on the prevalence of IPV. This analysis addressed the first research question detailed above; that is, what are the main effects of individual- and couple-level predictors on the prevalence of severe IPV against women? The overall findings of the level-one predictors are consistent with previous research on individual and couple correlates of IPV. As can be seen in Table 2, older males were significantly less likely to engage in IPV than were younger males, while males who reported substance use problems were more likely to engage in IPV than males who did not have substance use problems. Also in line with previous research was the finding that couples who earn high yearly incomes were less likely to experience partner violence, while couples characterized by unbalanced power in decision-making were more likely to experience violence. As demonstrated, 77 percent of the variation in IPV existed between individuals within neighborhood clusters. This indicates that while the majority of the occurrence of IPV exists at the individual and couple level, 23 percent of the variation in IPV exists at the neighborhood level.

Given the number of studies which show a strong effect of marital status (Stets, 1991; Yllo & Straus, 1981), race (e.g., Catalano, 2006; Caetano et al., 2008; Holtzworth-Munroe, Smutzler, & Bates, 1997), and employment status (e.g., MacMillian & Gartner, 1999) on IPV, it is somewhat surprising that only four variables in Table 2 reached significance. This may be due in part to hierarchical modeling techniques. For instance, the results presented in Table 2 have been adjusted for correlated error between the individuals within each NC (i.e., HLM recognizes that individuals are not independent of the neighborhood in which they reside). It may be that studies not adjusting for this shared error between individuals produce misleading results. Further, the findings could also be due to the outcome examined. As mentioned, the prevalence of severe violence measured here may capture primarily episodic couple violence. This type of violence may be particularly affected by situational factors, with only a few individual and couple factors being relevant. Certainly, that 23 percent of the variation in this type of IPV exists at the neighborhood level supports this argument. Nonetheless, the results presented in Table 2 are consistent with previous research regarding the predictors of IPV (e.g., Caetano et al., 2001, 2008; DeMaris et al., 2003; Kaufman Kantor & Straus, 1987; MacMillian & Gartner, 1999; Stith et al., 2004; Yount & Li, 2009).

Table 2: Random Coefficients Model Predicting the Prevalence of IPV[a]

Independent Variable	Coefficient	SE
Intercept	-1.600***	0.03
Level-One Independent Variables		
Male Age	-0.091**	0.04
Male Education[b]	-0.052	0.04
Male Hispanic[b]	-0.064	0.08
Male African American[b]	0.182	0.11
Male Unemployment	-0.084	0.12
Male Substance Use	0.515***	0.15
Female Substance Use	0.293	0.29
Female Social Isolation	0.043	0.05
Marital Status	0.167	0.11
Family Size	0.005	0.02
Income	-0.057**	0.03
Non-Democratic Views	0.208***	0.07
χ^2	36.08	
Proportion variation within NCs	0.77	

[a]Results are based on 3,235 individuals within 80 neighborhood clusters
[b]Coefficient does not vary significantly ($p \leq .05$) across neighborhood clusters
**$p \leq .05$ ***$p \leq .01$ (2-tailed)

Level-Two Main Effects: Structural Characteristics

Tables 3 through 11 present the results from the intercepts-as-outcome models for the prevalence of IPV. These models examined the main effects of neighborhood characteristics on the prevalence rates of severe female IPV victimization; recall that these models estimated neighborhood effects on rates of IPV after level-one predictors had been controlled. Table 3 addresses the second research question raised in this study; namely, controlling for individual- and couple-level predictors, what are the main effects of neighborhood concentrated disadvantage, immigrant concentration, and residential stability on neighborhood prevalence rates of IPV?

As demonstrated, concentrated disadvantage and immigrant concentration significantly affected prevalence rates of IPV, even after factors such as age, substance use, and income were controlled. Specifically, higher levels of neighborhood concentrated disadvantage increased the rates of IPV within those neighborhoods, while higher concentrations of immigrants within a neighborhood cluster actually decreased the prevalence rates of IPV. Residential stability did not significantly affect neighborhood IPV prevalence rates.

These findings are consistent with previous research assessing neighborhood effects on IPV. Miles-Doan (1998), Benson et al. (2000, 2003), Browning (2002), Van Wyk et al. (2003), Lauritsen and Schaum (2004), and Wright and Benson (2010) have all found that measures of concentrated disadvantage are significantly positively related to neighborhood IPV. Each of these researchers has suggested that concentrated disadvantage creates neighborhood conditions which are conducive to crime-related activities, such as assault and violence between strangers, and likewise, non-strangers such as intimates. Based on the evidence provided in Table 3, such an argument is supported.

The finding that immigrant concentration reduces partner violence is also consistent with a growing body of research; Lauritsen (2001) found that immigrant concentration reduced violent victimization within cities, while Desmond and Kubrin (2009) reported that immigrant concentration reduced neighborhood adolescent violence. Sampson et al. (2005) found that Latino violence was 10 percent lower than Caucasian violence, and they reported that first and second generation immigrations were less likely than older immigrants (e.g., third generation) to engage in violence. Martinez and Lee (2000) have also demonstrated that immigrants have lower homicide rates in Miami than non-immigrant populations. It is important to stress that while the negative impact of immigrant concentration is not expected by social disorganization theory, it is consistent with recent research regarding immigrants and crime. Finally, that residential stability did not significantly affect neighborhood IPV is also consistent with previous research. Browning (2002) and Lauritsen (2001) reported no significant effect of residential stability on neighborhood IPV. Although it is insignificant, the negative relationship between residential stability and the prevalence rate of IPV is nevertheless in the expected direction.

Table 3: Level-Two (Structural Characteristics) Main Effects on the Prevalence of IPV (Level-One Intercepts as Outcomes)[a]

Variables	B	SE
Intercept	-1.562***	0.04
Level-Two Variables		
Concentrated Disadvantage	0.120*	0.07
Concentrated Immigration	-0.115**	0.05
Residential Stability	-0.060	0.04
χ^2	31.76	
Proportion variation existing between NCs	0.23	

[a]Based on 80 neighborhood clusters
*$p \leq .10$ **$p \leq .05$ ***$p \leq .01$ (2-tailed)

Level-Two Main Effects: Collective Efficacy

Table 4 presents the effects of collective efficacy, as well as concentrated disadvantage, concentrated immigration, and residential stability, on the prevalence rate of IPV. These analyses, as well as the ones that follow in Tables 5 through 11, address the third research question posed by this study; that is, controlling for individual- and couple-level effects on the prevalence of IPV, what are the combined effects of neighborhood structural characteristics and neighborhood social mechanisms on rates of IPV? From a social disorganization standpoint, such a question asks whether the effects of neighborhood concentrated disadvantage, residential stability, and immigrant concentration on IPV are mediated by social mechanisms such as collective efficacy. As demonstrated in Table 4, introducing collective efficacy into model 2 rendered the effect of concentrated disadvantage on the IPV prevalence rate insignificant. However, the introduction of collective efficacy actually increased the size and significance level of the effect of concentrated immigration.

Although he did not use hierarchical modeling, Browning (2002) also found that collective efficacy significantly reduced nonlethal partner violence against females, and reduced the effect of concentrated disadvantage to insignificance; Browning (2002) also noted that residential stability and immigrant concentration were not significantly related to IPV. The results presented in Table 4 support some of Browning's (2002) findings. Although it was not significantly predictive of the prevalence rate of IPV when added to the multivariate Bernoulli model, collective efficacy did reduce the effect of concentrated disadvantage on IPV to insignificance; additionally, the direction of the relationship between collective efficacy and IPV rates was negative, which is in the predicted direction. However, contrary to Browning's (2002) results, concentrated immigration was highly predictive of lower prevalence rates of IPV.

Due to collinearity between concentrated disadvantage and collective efficacy, concentrated disadvantage was removed from model 3. Once concentrated disadvantage was dropped, collective efficacy became a significant ($p \leq .05$) predictor of neighborhood IPV rates and the effect of concentrated immigration remained essentially unchanged. These findings indicate that neighborhoods with higher concentrations of immigrants and higher levels of collective efficacy experienced lower prevalence rates of IPV. Based on these results, it appears that collective efficacy does influence non-street crimes, and is influential upon violence that occurs out of public view, such as the violence that occurs between partners.

Table 4: Level-Two (Collective Efficacy) Main Effects on the Prevalence of IPV (Level-One Intercepts as Outcomes)

Variables	Model 1 B	SE	Model 2 B	SE	Model 3 B	SE
Intercept	-1.562***	0.04	-1.562***	0.04	-1.563***	0.04
Level-Two Variables						
Concentrated Disadvantage	0.120*	0.07	0.081	0.07	--	--
Concentrated Immigration	-0.115**	0.05	-.0132***	0.05	-0.145***	0.06
Residential Stability	-0.060	0.04	-0.041	0.04	-0.043	0.05
Collective Efficacy	--	--	-0.257	0.19	-0.387**	0.19
χ^2	31.76		33.81		34.56	
Proportion variation existing between NCs					0.23	

*$p \leq .10$ **$p \leq .05$ ***$p \leq .01$ (2-tailed)

Level-Two Main Effects: Neighborhood Ties

Tables 5 and 6 present the effects of neighborhood social network interaction and social ties, respectively, on the prevalence rates of IPV. Overall, the findings suggest that neighborhood ties do not significantly impact the prevalence rates of severe intimate partner violence against females. These findings run counter with previous research indicating that social isolation is a risk factor for IPV (e.g., Stets, 1991; Van Wyk et al., 2003). However, the results may be due to the nature of IPV examined – specifically, the prevalence of partner violence. It is plausible that this type of violence is not severe enough for victims to activate social ties for help. From a social disorganization standpoint, then, it appears that neighborhood ties do not impact neighborhood control regarding episodic partner violence.

Social Network Interaction

As shown in Table 5, social network interaction rendered the effect of concentrated disadvantage on IPV insignificant when added to model 2, but did not change the effect of concentrated immigration. As with previous analyses reported here, residential stability was not a significant predictor of neighborhood IPV. Although social network interaction was not a significant predictor in this model, its positive direction is consistent with research conducted by Browning et al. (2004).

Table 5: Level-Two (Social Network Interaction) Main Effects on the Prevalence of IPV (Level-One Intercepts as Outcomes)

Variables	Model 1 B	SE	Model 2 B	SE
Intercept	-1.562***	0.04	-1.562***	0.041
Level-Two Variables				
Concentrated Disadvantage	0.120*	0.07	0.117	0.07
Concentrated Immigration	-0.115**	0.05	-0.110**	0.05
Residential Stability	-0.060	0.04	-0.060	0.04
Social Network Interaction	--	--	0.051	0.23
χ^2	31.76		32.48	
Proportion variation existing between NCs			0.23	

*$p \leq .10$ **$p \leq .05$ ***$p \leq .01$ (2-tailed)

Neighborhood Social Ties

Table 6 also reveals that neighborhood social ties are insignificant predictors of neighborhood prevalence rates of IPV. In fact, when added to model 2, which includes concentrated disadvantage, immigrant concentration, and residential stability, neighborhood social ties did not change any of the relationships among the structural predictors and rates of IPV. Higher levels of concentrated disadvantage continued to increase the likelihood of neighborhood IPV, while higher levels of immigrant concentrations significantly reduced this violence. Although not a significant predictor of IPV in the hierarchical model presented here, the negative relationship between neighborhood social ties and IPV prevalence rates is in the direction that would be expected by social disorganization theory.

Table 6: Level-Two (Social Ties) Main Effects on the Prevalence of IPV (Level-One Intercepts as Outcomes)

Variables	Model 1 B	Model 1 SE	Model 2 B	Model 2 SE
Intercept	-1.562***	0.04	-1.561***	0.04
Level-Two Variables				
Concentrated Disadvantage	0.120*	0.07	0.125*	0.07
Concentrated Immigration	-0.115**	0.05	-0.110**	0.05
Residential Stability	-0.060	0.04	-0.056	0.05
Social Ties	--	--	-0.021	0.10
χ^2	31.76		32.17	
Proportion variation existing between NCs			0.23	

*$p \leq .10$ **$p \leq .05$ ***$p \leq .01$ (2-tailed)

Level-Two Main Effects: Culture

Tables 7, 8, and 9 present the effects of cultural dimensions of neighborhoods on IPV prevalence rates across neighborhoods. Recall that these measures tap cultural aspects or cognitive landscapes of neighborhoods. Overall, the findings suggest that culture, especially legal cynicism, may be an important factor which influences neighborhood partner violence.

Tolerance for Deviance

Table 7 presents the effects of tolerance for deviance and neighborhood concentrated disadvantage, concentrated immigration, and residential stability on neighborhood IPV prevalence rates after controlling for individual- and couple-level effects. These findings are different from the previous findings regarding collective efficacy and neighborhood ties. Table 7 demonstrates that the inclusion of neighborhood tolerance for deviance reduced the effect of concentrated immigration on IPV rates to insignificance, but did not change the effect of concentrated disadvantage on IPV. It may be that tolerance of deviance within predominately immigrant neighborhoods negates the controlling effect of immigrant concentration on the occurrence of IPV. The positive relationship between tolerance for deviance and the prevalence rates of IPV is in line with Sampson and Bartusch's (1998) contention that neighborhood cognitive landscapes that are tolerant of deviance will experience more crime.

Legal Cynicism

Table 8 shows that legal cynicism, also a measure of neighborhood culture, was a significant ($p \leq .05$) predictor of IPV prevalence rates; it maintained a significant relationship with IPV even when placed in the same model as neighborhood disadvantage and immigration, as well as after individual- and couple-level predictors of IPV had been controlled. Legal cynicism also mediated the effect of concentrated disadvantage on IPV. Furthermore, when legal cynicism was added to the model, residential stability became a significant predictor of IPV.

Table 7: Level-Two (Tolerance for Deviance) Main Effects on the Prevalence of IPV (Level-One Intercepts as Outcomes)

Variables	Model 1 B	SE	Model 2 B	SE
Intercept	-1.562***	0.04	-1.566***	0.04
Level-Two Variables				
Concentrated Disadvantage	0.120*	0.07	0.130*	0.07
Concentrated Immigration	-0.115**	0.05	-0.077	0.05
Residential Stability	-0.060	0.04	-0.049	0.04
Tolerance for Deviance	--	--	0.234	0.14
χ^2	31.76		31.72	
Proportion variation existing between NCs			0.23	

*$p \leq .10$ **$p \leq .05$ ***$p \leq .01$ (2-tailed)

This finding is consistent with Warner and Pierce's (1993) contention that the inability for some residents to leave disadvantage areas breeds cynicism and anger. Table 8 indicates that while higher levels of neighborhood legal cynicism increased the prevalence rates of IPV, higher levels of concentrated immigration and residential stability reduced these rates. These relationships, with the exception of concentrated immigration, are consistent with expectations of the systemic disorganization model. Still, findings that concentrated immigration inhibit neighborhood IPV is in line with emerging research on immigration and general neighborhood crime (see Sampson & Bean, 2006).

Table 8: Level-Two (Legal Cynicism) Main Effects on the Prevalence of IPV (Level-One Intercepts as Outcomes)

Variables	Model 1 B	SE	Model 2 B	SE
Intercept	-1.562***	0.04	-1.561***	0.04
Level-Two Variables				
Concentrated Disadvantage	0.120*	0.07	0.103	0.07
Concentrated Immigration	-0.115**	0.05	-0.107**	0.05
Residential Stability	-0.060	0.04	-0.078**	0.04
Legal Cynicism	--	--	1.229**	0.55
χ^2	31.76		32.62	
Proportion variation existing between NCs			0.23	

*$p \leq .10$ **$p \leq .05$ ***$p \leq .01$ (2-tailed)

Satisfaction with Police

Table 9 indicates that satisfaction with the police was not a significant predictor of IPV prevalence rates. However, the inclusion of satisfaction with police into model 2 rendered the effect of concentrated disadvantage on IPV insignificant, but, as with collective efficacy (Table 4) and social network interaction (Table 5), it did not change the effect of concentrated immigration on neighborhood IPV rates.

Due to collinearity between satisfaction with the police and concentrated disadvantage, concentrated disadvantage was dropped from model 3. Concentrated immigration remained a significant predictor of IPV ($p \leq .05$) and residential stability became significant ($p \leq .10$). Satisfaction with police, however, continued to be insignificant.

According to Table 9, the relationships were in the expected direction – neighborhoods with higher levels of stability among residents and satisfaction with police experienced lower prevalence rates of IPV.

Table 9: Level-Two (Satisfaction with Police) Main Effects on the Prevalence of IPV (Level-One Intercepts as Outcomes)

Variables	Model 1 B	SE	Model 2 B	SE	Model 3 B	SE
Intercept	-1.562***	0.04	-1.560***	0.04	-1.561***	0.04
Level-Two Variables						
Concentrated Disadvantage	0.120*	0.07	0.090	0.08	--	--
Concentrated Immigration	-0.115**	0.05	-0.128**	0.05	-0.149**	0.06
Residential Stability	-0.060	0.04	-0.062	0.04	-0.070*	0.04
Satisfaction with Police	--	--	-0.142	0.22	-0.326	0.20
χ^2	31.76		32.62		33.11	
Proportion variation existing between NCs						0.23

*$p \leq .10$ **$p \leq .05$ ***$p \leq .01$ (2-tailed)

Level-Two Main Effects: Disorder

Tables 10 and 11 present the effects of physical and social disorder, respectively, on prevalence rates of intimate partner violence. Results indicate that physical disorder is an important neighborhood contributor to violence between partners.

Physical Disorder

Table 10 depicts the effects of physical disorder, concentrated disadvantage, concentrated immigration, and residential stability on prevalence rates of IPV, after level-one predictors have been controlled. Much like legal cynicism, physical disorder mediated the relationship between concentrated disadvantage and IPV rates. Moreover, physical disorder itself was a significant predictor ($p \leq .01$) of neighborhood IPV rates, while the effect of concentrated immigration was strengthened (to $p \leq .01$) when physical disorder was added to the analysis. Table 10 demonstrates that higher neighborhood levels of physical disorder increased prevalence rates of IPV, while, again, higher concentrations of immigrants reduced neighborhood IPV rates.

Table 10: Level-Two (Physical Disorder) Main Effects on the Prevalence of IPV (Level-One Intercepts as Outcomes)

Variables	Model 1 B	SE	Model 2 B	SE	Model 3 B	SE
Intercept	-1.562***	0.04	-1.557***	0.04	-1.557***	0.04
Level-Two Variables						
Concentrated Disadvantage	0.120*	0.07	0.020	0.07	--	--
Concentrated Immigration	-0.115**	0.05	-0.186***	0.05	-0.192***	0.06
Residential Stability	-0.060	0.04	-0.049	0.04	-0.051	0.04
Physical Disorder	--	--	0.203***	0.06	0.216***	0.07
χ^2	31.76		32.62		32.57	
Proportion variation existing between NCs					0.23	

*$p \leq .10$ **$p \leq .05$ ***$p \leq .01$ (2-tailed)

Collinearity between physical disorder and concentrated disadvantage necessitated that concentrated disadvantage be removed from model 3. Results remained unchanged even after concentrated disadvantage was removed. The consistency of results across models 2 and 3 suggest that the effects of concentrated immigration and physical disorder on IPV prevalence rates are real and meaningful; it appears that physical disorder in neighborhoods creates conditions which are conducive to or foster the eruption of violence between intimates.

Social Disorder

The effect of social disorder on IPV is provided in Table 11. Recall that because of the cost of coding data from videotapes in the Systematic Social Observation study, only 77 neighborhood clusters had viable information on social disorder; therefore, the analyses presented in Table 11 are based on all 77 NCs which provided information on social disorder.[19] According to Table 11, concentrated disadvantage, concentrated immigration, and residential stability were not significantly related to the prevalence rates of IPV across the 77 neighborhoods which had sufficient data on social disorder. Social disorder was also not a significant predictor of IPV. The insignificant effects of concentrated disadvantage and concentrated immigration in these 77 neighborhoods were surprising and not expected.

INCIDENCE OF INTIMATE PARTNER VIOLENCE

Tables 12 through 21 present the results from the hierarchical Negative Binomial models of the incidence of IPV. Recall that the incidence of IPV reflects the number of times during the past year that violence against a female intimate occurred; higher numbers on this variable indicate more frequent victimization. An exploratory analysis of the data indicated that the level-one predictors of the incidence of IPV were different from the significant predictors of the prevalence of IPV (the

---

[19] The level-one random coefficients model for these 77 NCs is presented in Appendix A.

Table 11: Level-Two (Social Disorder) Main Effects on the Prevalence of IPV (Level-One Intercepts as Outcomes)[a]

Variables	Model 1 B	SE	Model 2 B	SE
Intercept	-1.648***	0.04	-1.649***	0.04
Level-Two Variables				
Concentrated Disadvantage	0.083	0.07	0.127	0.08
Concentrated Immigration	-0.080	0.05	-0.059	0.05
Residential Stability	-0.043	0.04	-0.053	0.04
Social Disorder	--	--	-0.077	0.05
χ^2	33.465		34.02	
Proportion variation existing between NCs			0.22	

[a]Based on 77 neighborhood clusters
*$p \leq .10$ **$p \leq .05$ ***$p \leq .01$ (2-tailed)

specific results will be described later). However, these differences suggest that the incidence of IPV may capture a persistent form of partner violence. It was therefore relevant to examine whether the neighborhood-level predictors of this type of violence are different from those of the prevalence of IPV. The results presented next follow a similar format as those provided for the prevalence of IPV.

Level-One Random Coefficients Model

Table 12 depicts the results from the random coefficients Negative Binomial model; recall that this model involved estimating the individual- and couple-level (level-one) effects on the incidence of IPV. This analysis addressed the research questions regarding the main effects of individual- and couple-level predictors on the incidence of severe IPV against women. The overall findings of the level-one predictors are consistent with previous research on individual and couple correlates of IPV, and when compared to the findings from the level-one random coefficients Bernoulli model in Table 2, provide evidence that the two forms of IPV are indeed distinct.

Table 12 demonstrates that unemployed males and males who reported substance use problems engaged in violence towards their partners more frequently than men who were employed and reported no substance problems. Also in line with previous research was the finding that females who reported being socially isolated from friends or family members were significantly ($p \leq .01$) more likely to experience multiple victimizations from their partners. Regarding couple-level predictors of IPV, unmarried but cohabiting couples, couples with large families, and couples holding traditional or non-egalitarian views also experienced significantly more frequent violence, while couples earning high incomes engaged in IPV fewer times. These results are consistent with prior research (e.g., DeMaris et al., 2003; Kaufman Kantor & Straus, 1987; MacMillian & Gartner, 1999; Stets, 1991; Stith et al., 2004; Yount, 2005; Yount & Li, 2009).

The results here indicate that different factors predict the *frequency* of IPV than the *prevalence* of it. When compared to the findings in Table 2, four additional variables were significant for the incidence of IPV but not the prevalence of it. Specifically, unemployment, female social isolation, marital status, and family size were not significant predictors of the prevalence of IPV, but were significant for the incidence of IPV.

That more individual- and couple-level factors were predictive of the frequency at which IPV occurred than the prevalence of it suggests that the two outcomes may indeed tap different forms of violence. Further, the differences across the level-one findings for the two measures suggest that the incidence of IPV is a more individual-level phenomenon than is the prevalence of IPV. Such a conclusion is supported by the different amounts of variation in each outcome which exist at the individual/couple and neighborhood levels. Ninety-two percent of the variation in the incidence of IPV exists between individuals within neighborhood clusters, while 77 percent of the variation in the prevalence of IPV exists between individuals; this means that only 8 percent of the variation in the frequency of IPV and 23 percent of the variation in the prevalence of IPV exists at the neighborhood level. Clearly, the frequency at which IPV occurs between couples is more reliant upon individual- and couple-level factors. It may be that patterned and frequent violence between partners is more attributable to individual-level phenomena, such as frustration, stress, or low support, than is the occurrence of episodic violence. The fact that more level-one predictors were significantly related to the incidence of IPV rather than the prevalence of it supports this contention. Also, since less variation in the incidence of IPV exists at level-two, it may be expected that fewer neighborhood characteristics will be influential on this type of behavior.

Level-Two Main Effects: Structural Characteristics

Tables 13 through 21 present the results from the intercepts-as-outcome models for the incidence of IPV analyses. Recall that the intercepts-as-outcome models were used to examine the main effects of neighborhood characteristics on neighborhood rates of severe female victimization after level-one predictors were controlled. Table 13 assessed the main effects of neighborhood concentrated disadvantage, immigrant concentration, and residential stability on incidence rates of IPV after controlling for individual- and couple-level predictors.

Whereas concentrated disadvantage and concentrated immigration significantly influenced the prevalence rate of IPV, Table 13 shows that only concentrated immigration was significantly related ($p \leq .10$) to the incidence rate of IPV after individual- and couple-level factors were controlled. Specifically, higher levels of concentrated immigration were associated with lower frequency rates of IPV across neighborhoods. Again, while this relationship is not expected under the systemic social disorganization model, it is consistent with previous analyses presented in this study, as well as with the aforementioned work of Desmond and Kubrin (2009), Lauritsen (2001), Martinez and Lee (2000), Sampson et al. (2005), and Wright and Benson (2010). Also consistent with findings presented here is that residential stability was not significantly related to neighborhood IPV rates. Interestingly, concentrated disadvantage was not predictive of incidence rates of IPV, although it was predictive of the prevalence rates of IPV. Given the results in Table 13, it does not appear that neighborhoods of concentrated disadvantage foster persistent severe violence between partners.

Table 12: Random Coefficients Model Predicting the Incidence of IPV[a]

Independent Variable	Coefficient	SE
Intercept	-0.834***	0.08
Level-One Independent Variables		
Male Age	0.088	0.08
Male Education[b]	0.012	0.09
Male Hispanic[b]	0.016	0.16
Male African American[b]	0.235	0.22
Male Unemployment	0.452**	0.19
Male Substance Use[b]	1.047***	0.12
Female Substance Use[b]	0.370	0.23
Female Social Isolation	0.265***	0.07
Marital Status[b]	0.585***	0.19
Family Size	0.093***	0.03
Income	-0.331***	0.04
Non-Democratic Views	0.580***	0.10
χ^2	89.70	
Proportion variation existing within NCs	0.92	

[a] Results are based on 3,235 individuals within 80 neighborhood clusters
[b] Coefficient does not vary significantly ($p \leq .05$) across neighborhood clusters
**$p \leq .05$ ***$p \leq .01$ (2-tailed)

Table 13: Level-Two (Structural Characteristics) Main Effects on the Incidence of IPV (Level-One Intercepts as Outcomes)

Variables	B	SE
Intercept	-0.778***	0.09
Level-Two Variables		
Concentrated Disadvantage	0.045	0.13
Concentrated Immigration	-0.231*	0.13
Residential Stability	-0.032	0.10
χ^2		87.12
Proportion variation existing between NCs		0.08

*$p \leq .10$ **$p \leq .05$ ***$p \leq .01$ (2-tailed)

Level-Two Main Effects: Collective Efficacy

The analyses presented in Tables 14 through 21 examine the combined effects of neighborhood structural characteristics and neighborhood social mechanisms on the neighborhood incidence rates of IPV after level-one effects are controlled. Table 14 presents the effects of the structural variables and collective efficacy on the incidence rates of IPV.

Results indicate that collective efficacy is predictive ($p \leq .01$) of the incidence rates of IPV. Additionally, the introduction of collective efficacy to model 2 increased the significance level of concentrated immigration. According to Table 14, then, neighborhoods with higher levels of collective efficacy and higher concentrations of immigrants experienced significantly fewer occurrences of severe partner violence.

These findings are consistent with Browning's (2002) findings regarding collective efficacy and IPV. While Browning (2002) did not use hierarchical linear modeling, he did find that collective efficacy significantly reduced nonlethal partner violence against females. Additionally, that concentrated immigration significantly reduced the frequency rates of IPV is consistent with earlier findings regarding the prevalence rates of IPV. Thus, it appears that concentrations of immigrants actually inhibit partner violence. The results also suggest that collective efficacy may be more effective at reducing more persistent levels of IPV against females, as opposed to occasional instances of violence.

Due to collinearity between concentrated disadvantage and collective efficacy, disadvantage was removed from model 3. Results remained relatively unchanged, with collective efficacy dropping in significance (to $p \leq .05$), and concentrated immigration remaining the same. Overall, the findings indicate that neighborhoods with higher concentrations of immigrants and higher levels of collective efficacy experience lower IPV rates. The negative relationship between collective efficacy and IPV is theoretically expected.

Table 14: Level-Two (Collective Efficacy) Main Effects on the Incidence of IPV (Level-One Intercepts as Outcomes)

Variables	Model 1 B	SE	Model 2 B	SE	Model 3 B	SE
Intercept	-0.778***	0.09	-0.800***	0.09	-0.806***	0.09
Level-Two Variables						
Concentrated Disadvantage	0.045	0.13	-0.115	0.13	--	--
Concentrated Immigration	-0.231*	0.13	-0.333**	0.13	-0.303**	0.13
Residential Stability	-0.032	0.10	0.040	0.10	0.048	0.10
Collective Efficacy	--	--	-1.150***	0.42	-0.954**	0.40
χ^2	87.12		86.80		85.826	
Proportion variation existing between NCs					0.08	

*$p \leq .10$ **$p \leq .05$ ***$p \leq .01$ (2-tailed)

Level-Two Main Effects: Neighborhood Ties

Tables 15 and 16 present the effects of social network interaction and social ties, respectively, on neighborhood incidence rates of IPV. Similar to the findings regarding the prevalence of IPV, Table 15 suggests that social network interaction does not significantly impact incidence rates of severe intimate partner violence. However, unlike the previous findings reported here, Table 16 indicates that neighborhood social ties are significantly predictive of the frequency at which IPV occurs across neighborhoods.

Social Network Interaction

When entered into the model with concentrated disadvantage, concentrated immigration, and residential stability, social network interaction failed to mediate any relationships between the structural variables and the incidence rate of IPV; it also failed to significantly predict the incidence rate of IPV by itself. The effect of concentrated immigration remained unchanged once social network interaction was added to the model, with neighborhoods characterized by high levels of immigrants experiencing lower incidence levels of partner violence. As with previous analyses, residential stability was not a significant predictor of IPV.

Neighborhood Social Ties

Table 16 reveals that neighborhood social ties significantly reduced the frequency levels of IPV across neighborhoods. Furthermore, including neighborhood social ties into model 2 rendered the effect of concentrated immigration insignificant, suggesting a mediating effect; however, given the small change in the coefficient of concentrated immigration, a true mediating relationship may not be evident here.
Such a relationship is expected by the systemic social disorganization model, though, and provides evidence that the theory does in fact apply to intimate partner violence. Based on the findings presented in Table 16, it might be expected that concentrated immigration works through neighborhood social ties to reduce the incidence levels of IPV. For

now, however, it is important to note that neighborhoods with high levels of social ties experienced fewer occurrences of IPV. Further, when compared to the importance of neighborhood social ties on the prevalence of IPV, it appears that social ties may be more relevant in reducing the levels of persistent IPV against females than episodic violence within relationships.

Table 15: Level-Two (Social Network Interaction) Main Effects on the Incidence of IPV (Level-One Intercepts as Outcomes)

Variables	Model 1 B	SE	Model 2 B	SE
Intercept	-0.778***	0.09	-0.801***	0.09
Level-Two Variables				
Concentrated Disadvantage	0.045	0.13	0.061	0.13
Concentrated Immigration	-0.231*	0.13	-0.255*	0.14
Residential Stability	-0.032	0.10	-0.008	0.10
Social Network Interaction	--	--	-0.458	0.34
χ^2	87.12		83.78	
Proportion variation existing between NCs			0.08	

*$p \leq .10$ **$p \leq .05$ ***$p \leq .01$ (2-tailed)

Table 16: Level-Two (Social Ties) Main Effects on the Incidence of IPV
(Level-One Intercepts as Outcomes)

Variables	Model 1 B	SE	Model 2 B	SE
Intercept	-0.778***	0.09	-0.798***	0.09
Level-Two Variables				
Concentrated Disadvantage	0.045	0.13	0.143	0.14
Concentrated Immigration	-0.231*	0.13	-0.198	0.13
Residential Stability	-0.032	0.10	0.045	0.10
Social Ties	--	--	-0.472**	0.24
χ^2	87.12		84.85	
Proportion variation existing between NCs			0.08	

$*p \leq .10$ $**p \leq .05$ $***p \leq .01$ (2-tailed)

Level-Two Main Effects: Culture

Tables 17, 18, and 19 present the effects of the cultural characteristics of tolerance for deviance, legal cynicism, and satisfaction with the police, respectively, on neighborhood incidence rates of IPV. Similar to the results regarding the prevalence of IPV, the findings here suggest that culture may be an important factor which influences the frequency of severe partner violence against females. However, unlike the prevalence results, neighborhood satisfaction with the police was a significant predictor of the incidence rates of IPV, while legal cynicism was not.

Tolerance for Deviance

Table 17 presents the effects of tolerance for deviance, neighborhood concentrated disadvantage, concentrated immigration, and residential stability on incidence rates of IPV after controlling for individual- and couple-level effects. Interestingly, once added to model 2, tolerance for deviance reduced the effect of concentrated immigration to insignificance, but was not itself a significant predictor of the incidence rate of IPV. These results parallel those of the prevalence of IPV. Again, it may be that cognitive landscapes which are tolerant of deviance in areas of concentrated immigration are particularly damaging to the control capacities of those neighborhoods, thus negating the effect of immigrant population on the frequency at which IPV occurs.

Table 17: Level-Two (Tolerance for Deviance) Main Effects on the Incidence of IPV (Level-One Intercepts as Outcomes)

Variables	Model 1 B	SE	Model 2 B	SE
Intercept	-0.778***	0.09	-0.783***	0.09
Level-Two Variables				
Concentrated Disadvantage	0.045	0.13	0.050	0.13
Concentrated Immigration	-0.231*	0.13	-0.201	0.13
Residential Stability	-0.032	0.10	-0.013	0.10
Tolerance for Deviance	--	--	0.236	0.27
χ^2	87.12		87.35	
Proportion variation existing between NCs			0.08	

*$p \leq .10$ **$p \leq .05$ ***$p \leq .01$ (2-tailed)

Legal Cynicism

The results of legal cynicism on the incidence rates of IPV were quite different from those found for the prevalence of IPV. Recall that legal cynicism was a significant ($p \leq .05$) predictor of the prevalence rate of IPV (see Table 8), suggesting that neighborhood cynicism created conditions which fostered the occurrence of partner violence. Results provided in Table 18, however, indicate that neighborhood legal cynicism does not significantly affect the frequency at which such violence occurs, nor does it alter the effects of neighborhood characteristics on the incidence rates of IPV. While not significant, the results do suggest that areas characterized by legal cynicism are at risk for experiencing higher incidence levels of IPV, which is theoretically expected. Again, areas of concentrated immigration experienced lower incidence rates of IPV than areas not characterized by high concentrations of immigrant populations. This effect remained consistent even after legal cynicism was introduced into the model; the consistency of the relationship between concentrated immigration and neighborhood IPV rates across the models presented thus far suggests that the effect is meaningful.

Table 18: Level-Two (Legal Cynicism) Main Effects on the Incidence of IPV (Level-One Intercepts as Outcomes)[a]

Variables	Model 1		Model 2	
	B	SE	B	SE
Intercept	-0.778***	0.09	-0.787***	0.09
Level-Two Variables				
Concentrated Disadvantage	0.045	0.13	0.024	0.13
Concentrated Immigration	-0.231*	0.13	-0.231*	0.13
Residential Stability	-0.032	0.10	-0.054	0.09
Legal Cynicism	--	--	1.611	0.99
χ^2	87.12		84.51	
Proportion variation existing between NCs			0.08	

$*p \leq .10$ $**p \leq .05$ $***p \leq .01$ (2-tailed)

Satisfaction with Police

While it was not a powerful predictor of the prevalence of IPV, Table 19 shows that satisfaction with the police was a significant predictor of the incidence rates of IPV. In addition, including satisfaction with police into model 2 increased the effect of concentrated immigration. The results from this model suggest that neighborhoods of concentrated immigration and higher levels of satisfaction with the police experienced significantly lower incidence rates of IPV.

That satisfaction with police was a significant predictor of IPV incidence rates was somewhat surprising, given that it did not maintain a significant relationship with the prevalence of IPV. However, the effect of police satisfaction is consistent with previous research and theorizing regarding IPV; for instance, Plass (1993) suggests that a general distrust of the justice system may make IPV victims less likely to seek help from the police in order to leave violent relationships. Conversely, it may be that areas which are satisfied with the police foster conditions which support residents' calls to the police for intervention, such as in the case of frequent violence between partners. The findings presented in Table 19 support this view.

Due to collinearity between satisfaction with police and concentrated disadvantage, concentrated disadvantage was dropped from model 3. Concentrated immigration remained a significant predictor of IPV ($p \leq .05$), but satisfaction with the police became insignificant. Even so, relationships were in the expected direction, where neighborhoods with higher levels of stability among residents and satisfaction with police experienced lower IPV rates.

Table 19: Level-Two (Satisfaction with Police) Main Effects on the Incidence of IPV (Level-One Intercepts as Outcomes)

Variables	Model 1 B	SE	Model 2 B	SE	Model 3 B	SE
Intercept	-0.778***	0.09	-0.781***	0.09	-0.788***	0.09
Level-Two Variables						
Concentrated Disadvantage	0.045	0.13	-0.144	0.14	--	--
Concentrated Immigration	-0.231*	0.13	-0.327**	0.14	-0.284**	0.13
Residential Stability	-0.032	0.10	-0.033	0.09	-0.013	0.09
Satisfaction with Police	--	--	-0.854*	0.45	-0.587	0.40
χ^2	87.12		85.42		84.77	
Proportion variation existing between NCs					0.08	

*$p \leq .10$ **$p \leq .05$ ***$p \leq .01$ (2-tailed)

Level-Two Main Effects: Disorder

Tables 20 and 21 present the effects of physical and social disorder, respectively, on incidence rates of intimate partner violence. Contrary to the findings of the prevalence of IPV, the results indicate that neither physical nor social disorder is a significant neighborhood contributor to the frequency of violence between partners.

Physical Disorder

Table 20 indicates that physical disorder was not a relevant predictor of incidence rates of IPV. Given its highly significant ($p \leq .01$) effect on the prevalence rates of IPV, it was surprising that physical disorder was not significantly related to incidence rates of IPV. However, such results may be expected in terms of episodic versus persistent violence. While areas of physical disorder may create conditions which foster the *occurrence* of episodic violence between partners, the results in Table 20 indicate that these conditions do not foster high *levels* of violence between intimates.

Collinearity between physical disorder and concentrated disadvantage necessitated that concentrated disadvantage be removed from model 3. Results remained unchanged; thus, it appears that, while a significant predictor of the prevalence of violence between couples, physical disorder is not relevant to persistent violence between couples.

Table 20: Level-Two (Physical Disorder) Main Effects on the Incidence of IPV (Level-One Intercepts as Outcomes)

Variables	Model 1 B	SE	Model 2 B	SE	Model 3 B	SE
Intercept	-0.778***	0.09	-0.738***	0.09	-0.759***	0.09
Level-Two Variables						
Concentrated Disadvantage	0.045	0.13	-0.035	0.15	--	--
Concentrated Immigration	-0.231*	0.13	-0.272**	0.13	-0.259**	0.13
Residential Stability	-0.032	0.10	-0.035	0.10	-0.032	0.10
Physical Disorder	--	--	0.111	0.16	0.080	0.14
χ^2	87.12		88.14		86.41	
Proportion variation existing between NCs					0.08	

*$p \leq .10$ **$p \leq .05$ ***$p \leq .01$ (2-tailed)

Social Disorder

The effect of social disorder on IPV incidence rates is provided in Table 21. Recall that only 77 neighborhood clusters had information on social disorder; therefore, the analyses presented in Table 21 are based on only the 77 NCs with information on social disorder.[20] Similar to the analyses presented above, concentrated immigration was significantly related to the incidence rates of IPV, and reduced the frequency at which such violence occurred. However, when added to model 2, social disorder was not a significant predictor of IPV, and concentrated immigration remained unchanged. This finding is consistent with previous findings regarding the prevalence rates of IPV.

Table 21: Level-Two (Social Disorder) Main Effects on the Incidence of IPV (Level-One Intercepts as Outcomes)[a]

Variables	Model 1 B	SE	Model 2 B	SE
Intercept	-0.765***	0.09	-0.762***	0.09
Level-Two Variables				
Concentrated Disadvantage	0.012	0.13	0.043	0.16
Concentrated Immigration	-0.281**	0.14	-0.275**	0.14
Residential Stability	-0.061	0.10	-0.075	0.10
Social Disorder	--	--	-0.053	0.14
χ^2	86.16		86.65	
Proportion variation existing between NCs			0.07	

[a]Based on 77 neighborhood clusters
*$p \leq .10$ **$p \leq .05$ ***$p \leq .01$ (2-tailed)

---

[20] The level-one random coefficients model for these 77 NCs is presented in Appendix B.

Summary

The results presented in this chapter, and summarized in Table 22, demonstrate that variation in IPV exists at the neighborhood level, suggesting that partner violence is not purely an individual-level phenomenon. In fact, several neighborhood characteristics were important predictors of violence between partners, even after individual- and couple-level factors had been controlled. Concentrated immigration emerged as the most consistent predictor of both the prevalence and incidence of IPV, and collective efficacy also influenced both outcomes. Partner violence rates were lower in neighborhood clusters characterized by high levels of immigrants and collective efficacy. Concentrated disadvantage, legal cynicism, and physical disorder increased the likelihood of IPV, but did not affect the levels at which IPV occurred. Finally, neighborhood social ties reduced the frequency of IPV, but not the prevalence of it. Based on these findings, it can be concluded that social disorganization theory is applicable to the study of IPV.

Table 22: Summary of Main Results

	Prevalence Of IPV	Incidence Of IPV
Level-One Variables		
Male Age	(-)	
Male Education		
Male Hispanic		
Male African American		
Male Unemployment		(+)
Male Substance Use	(+)	(+)
Female Substance Use		
Female Social Isolation		(+)
Marital Status		(+)
Family Size		(+)
Income	(-)	(-)
Non-Democratic Views	(+)	(+)
Level-Two Variables		
Concentrated Disadvantage	(+)	
Concentrated Immigration	(-)	(-)
Residential Stability		
Collective Efficacy	(-)	(-)
Social Network Interaction		
Social Ties		(-)
Tolerance for Deviance		
Legal Cynicism	(+)	
Satisfaction with Police		(-)
Physical Disorder	(+)	
Social Disorder		
Proportion Variation Within NCs	0.77	0.92
Proportion Variation Between NCs	0.23	0.08

CHAPTER SIX

THEORETICAL AND POLICY IMPLICATIONS

This study examined the impact of neighborhood context on the problem of intimate partner violence perpetrated against females, and used the social disorganization perspective as its major theoretical framework. The effects of neighborhood structural characteristics and social mechanisms (e.g., collective efficacy) were examined using hierarchical modeling techniques. Based on the results presented in Chapter Five, three major conclusions can be drawn regarding neighborhood context and intimate partner violence. First, the findings from this study suggest that single versus multiple instances of IPV may be qualitatively different forms of violence that occur between partners. The prevalence and incidence of IPV were predicted by different individual-, couple-, and neighborhood-level factors, which raises the possibility that the two measures should not be considered the same type of violence. These results indicate that certain neighborhood factors create conditions which foster *episodic* violence, while other factors are related to *persistent* violence between partners.

Second, the results presented here demonstrate that neighborhood characteristics *do* significantly impact both the prevalence and incidence of intimate partner violence, even after individual- and couple-level predictors have been controlled. Specifically, concentrated immigration appears to be the most consistent structural predictor of IPV, while collective efficacy, social ties, aspects of culture, and physical disorder are predictive of certain forms of IPV (e.g., prevalence and incidence). The findings regarding these neighborhood conditions were largely consistent with the expectations of social disorganization theory, indicating that disorganization theory can be applied to the study of partner violence even though it often occurs in private.

Finally, and perhaps most importantly, the findings from this study suggest that partner violence is not purely an individual-level phenomenon. That variation existed in IPV between neighborhoods for both incidence and prevalence models suggests that IPV is not wholly accounted for by individual- and couple-level factors such as age or income.

THE PREVALENCE AND INCIDENCE OF INTIMATE PARTNER VIOLENCE ARE QUALITATIVELY DIFFERENT

This study found that the individual-, couple-, and neighborhood-level predictors of the prevalence of IPV were different than the individual-, couple-, and neighborhood-level predictors of the incidence of IPV. That each outcome was affected by different factors suggests that the two measures may tap different forms of behavior. It has been argued throughout this study that the prevalence of IPV reflects primarily episodic violence, where violence erupts between individuals sporadically – at least one time during the past year – but does not occur repeatedly. The incidence of IPV, on the other hand, may reflect a patterned type of violent behavior perpetrated against females in the relationship.

This does not suggest that the incidence of IPV should be viewed as an indicator of patriarchal terrorism (see Johnson, 1995), since the methodology and definition of IPV used in this study were more likely to capture common couple violence than patriarchal terrorism. However, theory does not preclude the possibility that heterogeneity exists *within* common couple violence; in fact, this heterogeneity may produce the reported differences in the correlates of the prevalence and incidence measures of IPV. Although these two forms of IPV are considered common couple violence, they may nonetheless be different from one another. Methodological and substantial implications arise from these possibilities. Methodologically, it appears that how IPV is defined will influence conclusions regarding the importance of neighborhood context on partner violence. For instance, neighborhood characteristics were more influential on the prevalence of IPV than on the incidence of it; therefore, conclusions regarding the effects of neighborhood context may be overstated if researchers only examine the prevalence of IPV, while they might be understated if researchers

Theoretical and Policy Implications

only examine the incidence of IPV. Researchers should be aware of this potential impact on their findings. Related to this, it is important that neighborhood-level research consider both the prevalence and incidence of IPV.

Substantively, the results of this study suggest that couples who engage in repeated IPV may be qualitatively different than couples involved in sporadic violence. The results of this study support this argument. It appears that the incidence of IPV is more heavily influenced by individual and couple characteristics, such as unemployment status and social isolation, than is the prevalence of IPV. This conclusion is demonstrated by the number of significant level-one predictors for the incidence of IPV compared to the prevalence of IPV, as well as the amount of variation in IPV that exists at the individual- and couple-level for both outcomes. Specifically, while 8 percent of the incidence of IPV could be influenced by neighborhood characteristics, 23 percent of the prevalence of IPV could be affected by the same factors. It appears that at the individual level, stress, frustration, and isolation are particularly more important in predicting frequent violence than episodic violence. That is, couples who engage in repeated violence report more stress, frustration, and isolation than those who do not engage in IPV or who do so only once. These findings support the notion that the two forms of IPV are influenced by different factors, and arise under different circumstances. It is imperative that future research consider the differences between the types of violence examined here – is the prevalence of IPV different than the incidence as it has been suggested? If so, research should seek to understand how they are different, and how these differences may impact the findings of either individual- or neighborhood-level research in the intimate partner violence area.

Given these results, it is not surprising that various neighborhood characteristics also differentially predict the prevalence and incidence of IPV. Areas characterized by high levels of disadvantage, cynicism, and physical disorder appeared to foster episodic violence between partners, while areas characterized by high levels of immigrants, collective efficacy, social ties, and satisfaction with the police were more effective at controlling frequent violence against women.

It appears that the prevalence of IPV is influenced by many of the same neighborhood factors that affect general street violence. Concentrated disadvantage, collective efficacy, and physical disorder have been found to be predictors of street-level crime (e.g., Krivo & Peterson, 1996; Sampson et al., 1997; Wilson & Kelling, 1982) and legal cynicism has been theorized to be correlated with street violence (e.g., Sampson & Bartusch, 1998). The results of this study mirror these findings regarding street-level crimes: disadvantage, legal cynicism, and physical disorder increased the likelihood that IPV occurred, while collective efficacy functioned as a protective factor against the occurrence of partner violence.

While the above characteristics exacerbated one-time or sporadic violence between partners, they did not appear to foster persistent violence between partners. In fact, consistent with the notion that persistent violence is affected more by individual and couple characteristics, no neighborhood factors significantly increased this type of IPV. Instead, concentrated immigration, social ties, collective efficacy, and satisfaction with police *reduced* the incidence rate of IPV. I speculate that these variables are related to repetitive IPV because they promote intervention. That is, within these neighborhoods, when violence is persistent, victims may seek help in order to stop the violence or neighbors may be willing to intervene on their behalf. Indeed, areas with high concentrations of immigrants are said to be characterized by strong social ties (e.g., Desmond & Kubrin, 2009), and as such, may be more able to recognize when violence occurs between partners or may be more able to respond or intervene when necessary. The same argument may also be true of neighborhoods which have strong social ties between residents – victimized women may be more able or likely to seek help from others in the neighborhood to whom they have ties (e.g., Stets, 1991). Collective efficacy may also be negatively related to persistent IPV because neighbors are more likely to be watching out for one another and are willing to intervene on violence if necessary (e.g., Sampson et al., 1997). Finally, in neighborhoods where residents are largely satisfied with the police, the residents who are being victimized by IPV may be more likely to call the police for intervention because they trust that the police can or will help.

Theoretical and Policy Implications

Although each type of IPV appeared to be differentially predicted by individual-, couple-, and neighborhood-level factors, they did share two predictors. Immigrant concentration and collective efficacy were the only neighborhood variables which significantly impacted both IPV outcomes, suggesting that these factors are particularly important to consider when assessing neighborhood effects on partner violence. Further, these factors may be particularly important for policy considerations. While it would be impractical for interventions to attempt to recruit immigrants to certain neighborhoods, it would be practical to attempt to increase social control through collective efficacy. Neighborhoods might build collective efficacy by fostering interaction and communication between residents – for instance, neighborhoods that organize block parties or sponsor organizational meetings where residents can get together to discuss the problems and future goals of the neighborhood could foster interaction and collective efficacy among residents. Such measures in turn reduce the likelihood of violence in general as well as violence between partners in those neighborhoods.

NEIGHBORHOOD CHARACTERISTICS DO IMPACT INTIMATE PARTNER VIOLENCE

As noted above, the findings from this study indicate that neighborhood characteristics derived from social disorganization theory *do* impact the likelihood and frequency of intimate partner violence against females. Therefore, the results indicate that social disorganization theory does apply to non-street crimes such as partner violence. Although the prevalence and incidence of IPV appear to be largely influenced by individual- and couple-level factors, this study found that neighborhood characteristics, such as concentrated immigration, concentrated disadvantage, and collective efficacy, among others, were predictive of partner violence. Hence, social disorganization theory can be used to study the neighborhood effects on this type of violence.

Concentrated Immigration

Of the three structural characteristics examined in this study, concentrated immigration was the strongest and most consistent predictor of intimate partner violence. It was negatively related to both prevalence and incidence rates of IPV; that is, neighborhoods characterized by high concentrations of Latino and foreign-born residents were less likely to experience IPV (i.e., prevalence) and experienced fewer occurrences of IPV (i.e., incidence) than neighborhoods not characterized by high immigrant populations. This finding is a particularly strong one, given its consistency across both prevalence and incidence models. However, the negative effect of concentrated immigration is not expected by the systemic social disorganization model. Recall that this model posits that ethnic heterogeneity or immigrant concentration disrupts the control capacities of neighborhoods by impeding the formation and breadth of social ties between neighbors; the result is a lack of social ties between neighbors, which reduces the control and supervision capacities of the neighborhood (Bursik & Grasmick, 1993; Kornhauser, 1978).

The results of this study, however, suggest that concentrated immigration actually *increases* neighborhood control, especially in terms of the violence which occurs between intimates. This relationship is consistent with recent research (e.g., Desmond & Kubrin, 2009; Martinez & Lee, 2000; Martinez et al., 2004; Sampson, 2008; Sampson & Bean, 2006; Sampson et al., 2005) on neighborhood immigration population and street crime, and contributes to an intriguing body of research indicating that immigrant concentration may actually inhibit crime.

Various explanations can be given for why immigrant concentration reduces violence in neighborhoods. Scholars suggest that many immigrants settle where their family or friends have previously settled and this proximity with other immigrants creates social ties and social networks between residents (Chiswick & Miller, 2005; Desmond & Kubrin, 2009). Martinez et al. (2004) contend that the informal networks created in immigrant neighborhoods are particularly strong inhibitors to crime, and Desmond and Kubrin (2009) suggest that these networks increase human capital by providing employment and other

Theoretical and Policy Implications

opportunities which aid immigrants in their adaptation to the American way of life. Furthermore, they suggest that immigrant communities, in part through their strong ties and networks, are able to shield residents from the crime-inducing effects of American culture, disadvantage, and discrimination. Desmond and Kubrin go on to suggest that high levels of immigrants within neighborhoods build community cohesion among residents by preserving cultural norms and providing ethnic solidarity. Sampson et al. (2005) also propose that immigrants, especially Latinos, are more likely to live in two parent homes where the adults are married; they argue that such a family environment is an important protective factor against criminal involvement. These researchers have all found evidence of a "Latino paradox" (see Sampson, 2008; Sampson & Bean, 2006), where immigrant status, at both individual and macro-social levels, has a negative effect on crime.

Based on such evidence, Martinez and Lee (2000) suggest that concentrated immigration does not create disorganization, as is implied by the social disorganization model. Instead, they argue that immigrant concentration may stabilize neighborhoods by creating new social and economic institutions. They also contend that a revision to the social disorganization model is needed to account for this effect.

The findings from the study presented here suggest that, with regard to intimate partner violence, immigrant concentration is certainly a protective factor that inhibits both the prevalence and incidence rates of IPV. Borrowing from Chiswick and Miller (2005), Desmond and Kubrin (2009), Martinez et al. (2004), Sampson (2008), and Sampson et al. (2005), I speculate that high levels of immigration within a neighborhood reduce violence between couples because of the strength and breadth of ties between immigrants. If, as suggested by many scholars, social ties and networks between immigrants are strong, these social ties may provide more social control upon couples in primarily two ways. First, social ties may provide outlets for victims of partner violence to seek help, and second, social ties may increase the likelihood that violence becomes publically known. Either way, it is possible that immigration protects women from IPV at least in part through strong social ties.

Immigrant status may also shield residents from the crime-inducing effects of American culture by preserving their own ethnic cultures (Desmond & Kubrin, 2009). It has been suggested that recent immigrants are less violent than second- and third-generation immigrants (Martinez & Lee, 2000; Martinez et al., 2004; Sampson, 2008; Sampson et al., 2005). Thus, the regulatory effect of immigration on IPV found here may be due to cultural ideals – that is, that violence against women is culturally unacceptable. Such cultural beliefs may be stronger among immigrants who have only recently moved to America, or it may be particularly likely among immigrants from matriarchal societies. Whether the immigrants in this study were first-, second-, or third-generation immigrants was not examined here. However, in their assessment of ethnicity and crime among respondents of the PHDCN, Sampson et al. (2005) reported that a large portion of the Latino respondents in waves one through three of the project were either first- or second-generation immigrants. As such, it is possible that the "immigrant concentration" measure examined here reflects many recent immigrants.[21] Wright and Benson (2010) recently confirmed this expected relationship – they found that the effect of immigrant concentration on IPV rates was partially mediated by social ties with family members and cultural values that did not condone violence within families.

Finally, a greater cohesiveness among immigrants may result in community organized behavior, regardless of other community characteristics, such as collective efficacy. It appears that with the exception of neighborhood tolerance for violence and social ties, concentrated immigration is sufficiently strong to reduce IPV. The exact mechanisms regarding this effect (e.g., whether the effect is due to social ties or cultural beliefs) should continue to be examined by research in the future.

---

[21] Recall that the measure of concentrated immigration was derived from the 1990 census data; however, it is highly plausible that the sampled respondents of the PHDCN accurately reflect the population characteristics (e.g., immigrant status) throughout the census tracts in Chicago.

Concentrated Disadvantage

According to the systemic social disorganization model, concentrated disadvantage disrupts neighborhood control by fostering residential mobility, immigrant concentration, and social cultural isolation, which in turn disrupts the formation or breadth of social ties and weakens residents' bonds to mainstream values (Kornhauser, 1978). As discussed, and contrary to theoretical expectations, this study found that immigrant concentration inhibits IPV. However, this study also found support for the theoretical expectations of concentrated disadvantage; the results indicate that concentrated disadvantage does in fact increase the likelihood of IPV, with areas of concentrated disadvantage being more likely to experience severe partner violence than neighborhoods not characterized by concentrated disadvantage. Thus, this study supports research conducted by Miles-Doan (1998), Benson and his colleagues (2000, 2003; Van Wyk et al., 2003), and Lauritsen and her colleagues (Lauritsen & Schaum, 2004; Lauritsen & White, 2001). Each of these researchers found that neighborhood disadvantage increased the likelihood of IPV.

The majority of previous research on neighborhood effects on partner violence has assessed the prevalence of IPV, but not its incidence (e.g., Benson et al., 2000; Benson et al., 2003; Benson et al., 2004; Lauristen & Schaum, 2004; Lauristen & White, 2001; Van Wyk et al., 2003).[22] As mentioned, this body of research has found that concentrated disadvantage increases the prevalence of IPV. Based on these findings, it was assumed that concentrated disadvantage would be significantly related to *both* the prevalence and incidence of IPV. It was surprising, then, to find that concentrated disadvantage was only predictive of the prevalence of IPV, but not the incidence of it. The findings suggest that neighborhoods characterized by concentrated disadvantage create conditions that somehow foster episodic but not persistent violence between couples.

These results may be accounted for in different ways. First, social cultural isolation may account for the direct effect of concentrated

---

[22] Miles-Doan (1998) examined the incidence rates of officially reported spousal violence.

disadvantage on the prevalence of IPV. That is, concentrated disadvantage may affect episodic IPV in much the same way that it affects general stranger violence. Wilson (1987) suggested that the effect of disadvantage on street crime arises because of social cultural isolation; that is, residents in disadvantaged areas have no role models from whom to learn middle-class and mainstream values. With regard to IPV, then, residents living in disadvantaged neighborhoods may lack middle class role models from whom to learn that violence against partners is wrong.

Another possible explanation for the null effect of concentrated disadvantage on the frequency of IPV is that its effects are indirect. Specifically, living in disadvantaged areas may foster feelings of frustration, alienation, and isolation within individuals and couples (Ross & Mirowsky, 2009). Recall that indicators of such factors (e.g., unemployment, social isolation) were predictors of the incidence of IPV. Therefore, it may be theorized that concentrated disadvantage works through individual-level characteristics to influence IPV. Such conditioning effects were not examined in this study. However, it is theoretically plausible that concentrated disadvantage creates neighborhood conditions which foster violence between partners, primarily by working through individual- and couple-level factors such as substance use, unemployment, isolation, and income. Although these relationships have yet to be examined, it is possible that concentrated disadvantage directly influences the prevalence of violence between partners, but only indirectly affects its frequency.

Finally, the measure of concentrated disadvantage that was used in this study may also account for its weaker-than-expected relationship with IPV. The measure that was used was a "global" factor score derived from the 1990 census data. Benson and his colleagues (2003) have suggested that concentrated disadvantage may be important to violence between intimates only in the most extremely disadvantaged areas (see also Krivo & Peterson, 1996); that is, there may be a "tipping point" at which disadvantage becomes relevant to severe violence between partners. Benson and his colleagues (2003) have found that extreme concentrated disadvantage is predictive of the prevalence of IPV, but variation in disadvantage below the extreme level is not related to IPV. Therefore, the measure used in this study may become a more powerful predictor of IPV when only the most extremely disadvantaged areas are assessed. Such an exploration may prove informative in future research.

Several policy implications arise with the finding that neighborhood disadvantage fosters IPV. In particular, police officers patrolling these areas and who respond frequently to calls in such neighborhoods would benefit from extra training regarding how to appropriately respond to intimate partner violence. Further, these officers should be well acquainted with the service providers for domestic violence in or close to disadvantaged areas so that they can refer victims and offenders to the appropriate services when they respond to calls for help. Services for intimate partner violence, such as domestic violence shelters, "safe zones," access to counselors, access to safety officers, and access to safe places for children of violent families should be strategically located in disadvantaged areas, as these are the more likely areas to have high concentrations of IPV problems and would thus service the population most at-risk for experiencing IPV.

Residential Stability

Residential mobility is theorized to affect neighborhood crime primarily by impeding the formation of social ties between neighbors, which in turn, reduces the control and supervision capacities of the neighborhood (Bursik & Grasmick, 1993; Kornhauser, 1978); conversely, it is expected that residential stability helps to increase neighborhood control. The results from this study support this notion – neighborhoods characterized by higher levels of residential stability were less likely to experience IPV and experienced fewer instances of IPV. However, the effect of residential stability was often not significant. In fact, its effect was only significant in two of the prevalence models and was not significant in any of the incidence models.

The results suggest that residential stability is not a consistent neighborhood predictor of either the occurrence or frequency of IPV. While neighborhoods may benefit from stability in terms of general crime and deviance, it does not appear that violence between partners is affected. Although not a significant predictor, the negative impact of residential stability was theoretically expected; social disorganization theory, then, appears to be applicable to IPV in this regard.

Collective Efficacy

Sampson (2006) and his colleagues (e.g., Sampson et al., 1997) have contended that neighborhoods with high levels of collective efficacy, that is, cohesion among residents coupled with a willingness to intervene in problems, experience less street crime than neighborhoods with little or no collective efficacy. However, it has been argued that collective efficacy may be less effective at controlling crime if the criminal behavior occurs out of public view, such as in the case of IPV (Raudenbush & Sampson, 1999). The findings from this study do not support this view. Collective efficacy was negatively associated with the likelihood of IPV, demonstrating that collective efficacy *does* reach beyond street crime. Further, although important to both types of IPV, collective efficacy may be more effective at reducing the frequency at which IPV occurs – in this study, efficacious neighborhoods were particularly resistant of frequent or persistent IPV. These findings are consistent with Browning (2002), who also reported that collective efficacy significantly reduced both partner severe violence and partner homicide. Collective efficacy also mediated the effect of concentrated disadvantage on the prevalence rate of IPV, which is expected by social disorganization theory. Together, these results demonstrate that the influence of neighborhood characteristics reaches beyond street crimes to violence which occurs inside the home.

Although it was not examined here, there may be reason to expect that the effect of collective efficacy on IPV is contingent upon social ties. Specifically, due to the private nature of violence between partners, neighborhood social ties with the victim or perpetrator may be necessary in order to gain knowledge of the violence. Once the violence is publically known, collective efficacy may then be relevant for intervention purposes.

There are several things that communities can do to build collective efficacy, which, based on these and other results, will work to lower crime in the area. Since collective efficacy involves social cohesion and trust among residents, then practices which seek to build

Theoretical and Policy Implications

relationships and cohesion between neighbors might be a way to begin building collective efficacy. Community programs which attempt to engage residents in neighborhood planning and decision-making might increase the community's capacity and involvement of residents; additionally, those programs that attempt to increase residents' feelings of belonging to or ownership of the community may work to build cohesion between residents (e.g., Mazerolle et al., 2010). Block-parties or organizational groups which encourage resident's participation and social engagements may also increase the likelihood that residents get to know one another.

Social Network Interaction

Social disorganization is typically conceived as one of the major sources of neighborhood social problems such as crime, while its converse, social organization, is conceived as the solution to such problems. However, there are circumstances where socially organized neighborhoods may nonetheless experience high rates of crime. Browning et al. (2004) stipulated that social networks between neighborhood residents increase the willingness of residents to engage in social control, but simultaneously decrease the regulatory effects of such networks. In essence, Browning et al.'s (2004) model explains why socially organized neighborhoods can also have high crime rates; the mutual obligations that result from social networks between neighbors may reduce the inhibiting effects of collective efficacy. While Browning et al. (2004) and Wilkinson (2007) have found evidence that social network interaction between residents reduces the controlling effect of collective efficacy on street crimes, the results from this study indicate that such interaction between neighbors does not significantly affect violence between partners. Neither the prevalence nor incidence of IPV were significantly impacted by social network interaction.

A few explanations could underlie the null findings reported here. First, the measure of social network interaction may be limited because it was not tailored to the types of interaction that occur between couples. Instead, the measure used in this study reflected neighborly interactions such as attending parties, visiting on the street, asking questions regarding child rearing, and doing favors for one another. Better measures pertaining to couple-level interaction such as double-dating may be more relevant to the study of IPV than the measures that were used in this study. Second, it has been suggested that violent couples are more socially isolated than nonviolent couples (Stets, 1991). As such, social network interaction may not be relevant to examine regarding IPV, because such interaction does not apply to violent couples.

Finally, as suggested by Browning et al. (2004), social network interaction may be important to criminal outcomes when it weakens the effectiveness of collective efficacy in controlling such behavior. Browning et al. (2004) argued that mutual obligations created through social network interaction between law-abiding and law-violating residents reduce the control capacity of neighborhoods by reducing the regulatory effect of collective efficacy. Such a relationship between social network interaction and collective efficacy on neighborhood IPV rates was not examined here; however, it is theoretically plausible that social network interaction impacts neighborhood rates of IPV by weakening the effect of collective efficacy on partner violence. That is, efficacious neighborhoods where violent and nonviolent couples share mutual obligations may be less protected from IPV because the effect of collective efficacy is weak. While such a relationship was not assessed here, the direct effect of social network interaction was not meaningfully related to neighborhood IPV rates. This does not, however, discount the potential negative effect that social network interaction may have on the effect of collective efficacy on IPV rates. It is recommended that future research examines the potential inhibitory effect of social network interaction on the effect of collective efficacy.

Neighborhood Social Ties

Unlike social network interaction, neighborhood social ties do appear to reduce severe violence against females, especially the frequency of such violence. This study found that while neighborhood social ties did not significantly affect prevalence rates of IPV, they did reduce the incidence rates of IPV. That is, neighborhoods within which residents

Theoretical and Policy Implications 137

had many friends and family members living experienced significantly fewer incidences of partner violence against females. This effect is theoretically expected, both at the individual- as well as the neighborhood-levels. The systemic social disorganization theory stipulates that social ties foster a sense of community, which then leads to organized community behavior such reducing crime and victimization (e.g., Kasarda & Janowitz, 1974; Shaw & McKay, 1942). Social ties have also been theorized to increase neighborhood control through increased surveillance and supervision capacities (e.g., Bellair, 2000; Bursik & Grasmick, 1993), and to facilitate the transmission of values regarding acceptable behavior between residents (e.g., Warner, 2003). At the individual level, social ties are important to the prevention of and escape from violent relationships; women with few social ties may have few people to turn to for assistance in leaving the relationship, the violence is unlikely to be recognized or brought to the attention of others, and social control from outside parties is rarely exerted on isolated couples (e.g., Stets, 1991; Van Wyk et al., 2003). Thus, there is certainly reason to expect that social ties reduce the likelihood of IPV among couples.

The results from this study support the above arguments. Neighborhood social ties were most important in reducing the neighborhood frequency rates at which IPV occurred, but they were not significantly predictive of the prevalence rates of IPV. This finding may suggest that either sporadic violence (captured by the prevalence measure of IPV in this study) is more tolerable than frequent or persistent violence (captured by the incidence measure of IPV), or that the effect of neighborhood social ties is a reactive phenomenon. It may be that only when violence between partners becomes frequent, persistent, or patterned, social ties become important in reducing the violence. For instance, while social ties cannot prevent the first offense from occurring, they can inhibit subsequent offenses. Victims may activate neighborhood social ties for help in leaving the relationship or for intervention purposes, perpetrators may tell others about the violence, or it may become difficult for couples to hide the violence once it occurs often. In these ways, the effect of ties works through the mechanisms of supervision, surveillance, social control, and intervention. Individual social isolation may also interact with neighborhood social ties to exacerbate (or alleviate) IPV. That is, neighborhood social ties could condition the effect of individual social isolation on IPV. Although not examined in this study, cross-level interactions between neighborhood social ties and individual levels of social isolation may be used in future research to examine such relationships.

This study also found that social ties mediated the relationship between concentrated immigration and the incidence of IPV. This suggests that, in line with the systemic disorganization theory, the effect of concentrated immigration may work through neighborhood social ties to reduce the frequency at which partner violence occurs. As discussed above, areas characterized by high levels of immigrants are often also characterized by high levels of social ties between neighbors; this could be due to the fact that many immigrants and their families tend to live in the same neighborhoods (Chiswick & Miller, 2005; Desmond & Kubrin, 2009), or that such ties are necessary to facilitate immigrants' adaptation into American life (Martinez et al., 2004). Regardless of the explanation, the results presented here indicate that the regulatory effect of concentrated immigration on partner violence occurs through the strength of the ties among the residents.

Based on the results of this study, neighborhoods would most likely benefit from practices which attempt to increase or strengthen social ties between residents. It is important to caution, however, that building social ties between law-abiding and law-violating may inhibit social control (e.g., Browning et al., 2004). Still, social ties between residents can be crime-inhibiting, and neighborhoods may thus want to foster relationships among residents. In this regard, practices which encourage occasional interaction between residents could again be important. Neighborhood parties or organizational participation which gets residents together may help develop social ties. Additionally, neighborhoods should consider ways to maintain long-term residents, as residential turnover appears to inhibit and disrupt the formation of social ties (e.g., Kornhauser, 1978).

Tolerance for Deviance

Cognitive landscapes are theorized to affect neighborhood behavior by generating and fostering norms regarding appropriate behaviors (Sampson & Wilson, 1995). It is generally expected that neighborhoods with cognitive landscapes which are tolerant of deviance or those which are cynical of the law are more likely to experience street and violent crime. On the other hand, neighborhoods which have cognitive landscapes that reflect satisfaction with the police are less likely to have high crime rates (Sampson & Bartusch, 1998). The findings from this study support these expectations, and suggest that cognitive landscapes also influence non-street crimes, such as IPV.

The results from this study indicate that neighborhood tolerance for deviance reduced the effect of concentrated immigration on IPV. Thus, neighborhoods in which residents were tolerant of general deviance were not protected against IPV by immigrant population. This was a consistent finding across both prevalence and incidence models, and suggests that neighborhood tolerance for deviance may be particularly damaging in areas with high concentrations of immigrants. The results indicate that whereas concentrated immigration significantly reduces the occurrence and frequency of partner violence, including tolerance for deviance in the same model renders this effect insignificant. This suggests that the protection against partner violence that is provided by high levels of immigrants is undermined in neighborhoods where residents are generally tolerant of deviance.

Further, tolerance for deviance was the only neighborhood characteristic examined in this study which negated the effect of concentrated immigration on both outcome measures. Recall that concentrated immigration was the most powerful and consistent neighborhood predictor of IPV in this study; for tolerance of deviance to negate such an effect suggests that this type of cognitive landscape is particularly damaging to the control capacities that concentrated immigration provides for a neighborhood.

Although tolerance of deviance did not maintain a direct effect on partner violence, a better measure of neighborhood tolerance of *partner violence* may generate a stronger effect on IPV. The measure of tolerance of deviance used in this study reflected general deviant behaviors (e.g., underage drinking or smoking) and did not tap behaviors specific to violence between partners. It may be that measures relating more specifically to partner violence, such as hitting one's partner, may be particularly powerful neighborhood characteristics on IPV. Given the effect of tolerance for deviance found here, it could be expected that a more precise measure of neighborhood tolerance for violence between intimate partners would exert a stronger effect on IPV than was demonstrated in this study.

Legal Cynicism

This study found that cognitive landscapes characterized by cynicism of the legal and justice systems increase the likelihood that IPV will occur, but have no effect on the frequency at which IPV occurs. It is interesting that legal cynicism predicted the prevalence of IPV, but not the incidence of it. This may further support the notion that the two measures tap different forms of IPV, with the prevalence of IPV being a more general type of violence when compared to the incidence of IPV. In this regard, that legal cynicism increased the prevalence of IPV is consistent with theoretical expectations regarding legal cynicism and increased risk of street crime (e.g., Sampson & Bartusch, 1998).

Sampson and Bartusch (1998) suggested that neighborhood conditions, such as disadvantage, breed frustration, alienation, and cynicism among residents. In line with their reasoning, it is theoretically possible that areas which are characterized by legal cynicism breed frustration or foster conditions which make episodic violence (i.e., prevalence of IPV) between partners more likely, whereas such conditions do not provoke persistent violence between partners. In short, the frustration and cynicism experienced by neighborhood residents may result in occasional partner violence. Finally, distrust in the legal or justice systems may make neighborhoods less likely to call upon these service agencies for intervention purposes. In other words, legal cynicism may inhibit a neighborhood's willingness to mobilize itself for intervention or to organize itself for control purposes in order to regulate partner violence.

Satisfaction with Police

While neighborhood satisfaction with police performance does not appear to impact the prevalence of IPV, it does significantly reduce the frequency at which IPV occurs. Theoretically, it may be that more frequent or persistent violence necessitates formal intervention, such as that provided by the police. Therefore, neighborhoods which are satisfied with the police may facilitate police intervention because they foster a sense of trust between the residents and the police. Plass (1993) argued that a general distrust of the justice system may make IPV victims less likely to seek help from the police in order to leave the relationship or stop the violence; the findings of this study support a similar argument – areas which are characterized by satisfaction with the police experience lower levels of violence between partners. This could be due in part to residents' general trust in the police, which may make it more likely for victims or others to seek help from the police. It may be worth exploring in future research whether neighborhood satisfaction with police conditions residents' willingness to formally report IPV to the police or other service agencies.

Neighborhoods can attempt to decrease legal cynicism and increase satisfaction with the police among its residents, and this may reduce crime and intimate partner violence in these areas. One potential way that neighborhoods can do this is to foster positive interactions with the police and residents. This may involve encouraging police departments to use foot patrol more often in the area or implement a community-oriented style of policing so that officers can more easily interact with the residents. Neighborhoods may also try to organize a community watch program whereby the residents can work closely with the local police force. Finally, locating a police substation in neighborhoods characterized by high legal cynicism and low police satisfaction may also help to reduce negative feelings among the residents about police, the legal system, and the justice system.

Physical Disorder

Findings from this study reveal that physical disorder is a strong predictor of the prevalence of IPV, but has no impact on the incidence of IPV. The results suggest that neighborhoods characterized by high amounts of garbage, graffiti, and other physical signs of disorder create conditions which not only breed violence in general (e.g., Wilson & Kelling, 1982), but also foster episodic violence between couples. It may be that areas of physical disorder send signs to residents that neighborhood control is low or ineffective (Ross et al., 2001; Ross & Mirowsky, 2009). Additionally, living in areas that are physically dilapidated, unkempt, and disregarded may foster frustration and anger among residents, which can result in outbursts of violence between partners. In this way, physical disorder may also impact IPV *indirectly*, as well as directly. That physical disorder was not predictive of the incidence of IPV not only provides support that the incidence is qualitatively different than the prevalence of IPV, but also indicates that physical disorder does not foster persistent violence against female intimates. Although the relationship between disorder and collective efficacy, as explored by Sampson and Raudenbush (1999), was not examined here, it is possible that the effect of disorder on IPV was due to a lack of collective efficacy. The results presented here only demonstrate that physical disorder does indeed increase the likelihood that partner violence will occur.

Social Disorder

Social disorder was not predictive of either the prevalence or incidence rates of IPV. These findings may be an artifact of data limitations. Fewer neighborhood clusters (i.e., 77 NCs instead of 80 NCs) had sufficient data regarding social disorder, which limited the number of neighborhoods assessed for these analyses. Additionally, social disorder is a slightly less robust scale than the physical disorder scale, consisting of only 7 indicators, as opposed to the 10 indicators which comprise the physical disorder scale (see Raudenbush & Sampson, 1999 for details regarding each scale); as such, the social disorder scale may be a weaker measure of disorder. Still, it could be that drinking and drug use, prostitution, fighting, and other socially deviant behaviors simply do not impact the violence that occurs between partners, even though physical disorder does.

INTIMATE PARTNER VIOLENCE IS NOT SOLELY AN INDIVIDUAL-LEVEL PHENOMENON

The findings regarding the prevalence and incidence of IPV indicate that there is variation in partner violence that exists outside of the individuals and couples who engage in such behavior. Specifically, 77 percent and 92 percent of the variation in the prevalence and incidence of IPV, respectively, exists within individuals or between couples. This means that 23 percent and 8 percent, respectively, of the variation in each form of violence exists outside of individuals and couples. These figures demonstrate that intimate partner violence against females is not solely an individual-level phenomenon; it can be explained in part by factors outside of individuals, such as by neighborhood characteristics.

This finding is an important one, considering the amount of research that has focused on individual-level predictors of partner violence. This study demonstrated that neighborhood context does influence IPV; as such, studies not considering contextual influences on partner violence may be limited in their explanatory power. Additionally, it is possible that the effect of neighborhood characteristics on IPV reported here are weaker than their *potential* effects. For instance, neighborhood measures tailored more specifically to IPV (e.g., tolerance for violence against partners), instead of general crime, may exert stronger influences on partner violence than were reported here. Also, it is plausible that neighborhoods *condition* the effects of certain predictors of IPV (e.g., social isolation); if so, the argument for examining neighborhoods and IPV becomes even stronger. The finding that 23 percent and 8 percent of the variation in the prevalence and incidence of IPV, respectively, exists at the neighborhood level certainly opens additional avenues for theoretical and practical explorations.

Summary

Previous researchers argued that IPV was not purely an individualistic phenomenon, and they demonstrated that neighborhood structural characteristics, such as disadvantage, were related to IPV (e.g., Benson et al., 2000, 2003; Lauritsen & Schaum, 2004; Lauritsen & White, 2001; Miles-Doan, 1998). Their findings presented initial evidence that IPV was influenced by sociological factors. While innovative and progressive, unfortunately, data limitations hindered their research endeavors in a couple of ways.

First, most of the aforementioned research used pooled regression techniques and were unable to employ hierarchical analyses to examine the effects of neighborhood characteristics on IPV. Therefore, prior research was unable to adjust for the problems created by correlated error, heteroskedasticity, and biased hypothesis tests when examining individual-, couple-, and neighborhood-level effects on IPV. The usefulness of hierarchical modeling techniques over pooled regression analyses was discussed, and it was argued that hierarchical analyses provide more accurate estimates of neighborhood effects on IPV after controlling for individual- and couple-level effects.

After using hierarchical modeling techniques to adjust for the problems of pooled regression, this study found that over 70 percent of the variation in IPV exists at the individual and couple level. These findings support Lauritsen and her colleagues' (Lauritsen & White, 2001; Lauritsen & Schaum, 2004) contention that a large portion of the relationship between community context and IPV is explained by individual and/or couple factors. While consistent with Lauritsen's expectations, this study found that there was still variation in IPV that existed at the neighborhood level. As such, it was concluded that intimate partner violence against females is not solely attributable to individual- and couple-level factors. In fact, the results of this study indicate that concentrated immigration, neighborhood social ties, aspects of culture, and physical disorder are neighborhood characteristics which influence violence between partners.

Finally, previous researchers were also unable to examine the effects of the neighborhood social mechanisms (e.g., collective efficacy) which are theorized to mediate the relationships between structural variables and neighborhood crime. Large datasets such as the NCVS and the NSFH do not provide information relating to collective efficacy, neighborhood social ties, or cognitive landscapes; this limited the sociological variables accessible to Benson, Lauritsen, and their colleagues to the structural predictors of IPV, such as disadvantage or

Theoretical and Policy Implications

poverty. The only research to date regarding neighborhood social intervening mechanisms and IPV was conducted by Browning (2002). Browning (2002) examined neighborhood collective efficacy on IPV, but did not use HLM analyses and did not use the same PHDCN data examined here. This study therefore extended research conducted by Benson, Browning, Lauritsen, and Miles-Doan regarding the effects of neighborhood factors on IPV. It also took additional steps to address the limitations of their work, such as examining social mechanisms with HLM techniques. The results of this endeavor compliment their research – neighborhood structural factors as well as intervening mechanisms do impact neighborhood rates of partner violence. It can now be concluded that IPV is not solely an individual-level phenomenon *and* that neighborhood elements (both structural and social) drawn from social disorganization theory are relevant predictors of partner violence. It is hoped that this study has taken steps in discerning the importance of such factors on the violence that occurs between partners.

APPENDIX A

Random Coefficients Model Predicting the Prevalence of IPV[a]

Independent Variable	Coefficient	SE
Intercept	-1.667***	0.03
Level-One Independent Variables		
Male Age	-0.099**	0.05
Male Education[b]	-0.071**	0.04
Male Hispanic[b]	-0.072	0.08
Male African American[b]	0.180	0.11
Male Unemployment	-0.033	0.12
Male Substance Use	0.534***	0.15
Female Substance Use	0.364	0.30
Female Social Isolation[b]	-0.013	0.03
Marital Status	0.184	0.11
Family Size	0.002	0.02
Income	-0.052	0.03
Non-Democratic Views	0.203***	0.07
χ^2	35.802	
Proportion variation within NCs	0.78	

[a]Results are based on 3,147 individuals within 77 neighborhood clusters
[b]Coefficient does not vary significantly ($p \leq .05$) across neighborhood clusters

**$p \leq .05$ ***$p \leq .01$ (2-tailed)

APPENDIX B

Random Coefficients Model Predicting the Incidence of IPV[a]

Independent Variable	Coefficient	SE
Intercept	-0.830***	0.09
Level-One Independent Variables		
Male Age	0.088	0.08
Male Education[b]	0.024	0.09
Male Hispanic[b]	0.001	0.16
Male African American[b]	0.222	0.22
Male Unemployment	0.396**	0.18
Male Substance Use[b]	1.039***	0.12
Female Substance Use[b]	0.518**	0.21
Female Social Isolation	0.274***	0.07
Marital Status[b]	0.596***	0.20
Family Size	0.097***	0.03
Income	-0.337***	0.04
Non-Democratic Views	0.603***	0.10
χ^2	89.02	
Proportion variation within NCs	0.93	

[a] Results are based on 3,147 individuals within 77 neighborhood clusters

[b] Coefficient does not vary significantly ($p \leq .05$) across neighborhood clusters

**$p \leq .05$ ***$p \leq .01$ (2-tailed)

REFERENCES

Anderson, E. (1999). *Code of the street: Decency, violence, and the moral life of the inner city*. New York: Norton & Co.

Archer, J. (2000). Sex differences in aggression between heterosexual partners: A meta-analytic review. *Psychological Bulletin, 126*(5), 651-680.

Atkinson, M. P., Greenstein, T. N., & Lang, M. M. (2005). For women, breadwinning can be dangerous: Gendered resource theory and wife abuse. *Journal of Marriage and the Family, 67*(4), 1137-1148.

Bachman, R., & Saltzman, L. E. (1995). *Violence against women: Estimates from the redesigned survey* (No. No. NCJ-154348). Washington, DC: Bureau of Justice Statistics Special Report, U.S. Department of Justice.

Baumer, E., Horney, J., Felson, R., & Lauritsen, J. L. (2003). Neighborhood disadvantage and the nature of violence. *Criminology, 41*(1), 39-71.

Bellair, P. E. (1997). Social interaction and community crime: Examining the importance of neighbor networks. *Criminology, 35*(4), 677-704.

Bellair, P. E. (2000). Informal surveillance and street crime: A complex relationship. *Criminology, 38*(1), 137-170.

Benson, M. L., Fox, G. L., DeMaris, A. A., & Van Wyk, J. (2000). Violence in families: The intersection of race, poverty, and community context. In G. L. Fox & M. L. Benson (Eds.), *Contemporary perspectives in family research: Families, crime and criminal justice* (Vol. 2, pp. 91-109). New York: Elsevier Science Inc.

Benson, M. L., Fox, G. L., DeMaris, A. A., & Van Wyk, J. (2003). Neighborhood disadvantage, individual economic distress and violence against women in intimate relationships. *Journal of Quantitative Criminology, 19*(3), 207-235.

Benson, M. L., Wooldredge, J. D., Thistlethwaite, A. B., & Fox, G. L. (2004). The correlation between race and domestic violence is confounded with community context. *Social Problems, 51*(3), 326-342.

Bernburg, J.G., & Thorlindsson, T. (2007). Community structure and adolescent delinquency in Iceland: A contextual analysis. *Criminology, 45*(2), 415-444.

Browning, C. R. (2002). The span of collective efficacy: Extending social disorganization theory to partner violence. *Journal of Marriage and the Family, 64*(4), 833-850.

Browning, C. R., Feinberg, S. L., & Dietz, R. D. (2004). The paradox of social organization: Networks, collective efficacy, and violent crime in urban neighborhoods. *Social Forces, 83*(2), 503-534.

Browning, C.R., & Olinger-Wilbon, M. (2003). Neighborhood structure, social organization, and number of short-term sexual partnerships. *Journal of Marriage and Family, 65*, 730-745.

Brush, L. D. (1990). Violent acts and injurious outcomes in married couples: Methodological issues in the National Survey of Families and Households. *Gender & Society, 4*, 56-67.

Bursik, R. J. (1988). Social disorganization and theories of crime and delinquency: Problems and prospects. *Criminology, 26*(4), 519-551.

Bursik, R. J., & Grasmick, H. G. (1993). *Neighborhoods and crime*. Lanham: Lexington.

Bursik, R. J., & Webb, J. (1982). Community change and patterns of delinquency. *The American Journal of Sociology, 88*(1), 24-42.

Byrne, J. M., & Sampson, R. J. (Eds.). (1986). *The social ecology of crime*. New York: Sprinter-Verlag.

Caetano, R., Schafer, J., & Cunradi, C. (2001). Alcohol-related intimate partner violence among white, black, and Hispanic couples in the United States. *Alcohol Research and Health, 25*(1), 58-65.

Caetano, R., Vaeth, P.A.C., Ramisetty-Miler, S. (2008). Intimate partner violence victim and perpetrator characteristics among couples in the United States. *Journal of Family Violence, 23*, 507-518.

Carr, P. J., Napolitano, L., & Keating, J. (2007). We never call the cops and here is why: A qualitative examination of legal cynicism in three Philadelphia neighborhoods. *Criminology, 45*(2), 445-480.

Catalano, S. (2006). *Intimate partner violence in the United States*. Washington, DC: US Department of Justice.

Catalano, S., Smith, E., Snyder, H., & Rand, M. (2009). *Female victims of violence* (No. NCJ-228356). Washington, DC: Bureau of Justice Statistics.

Chiswick, B.R., & Miller, P.W. (2005). Do enclaves matter in immigrant adjustment? *City and Community, 4*, 5-35.

Clements, C.M., Oxtoby, C., & Ogle, R.L. (2008). Methodological issues in assessing psychological adjustment in child witnesses of intimate partner violence. *Trauma, Violence, & Abuse, 9*(2), 114-127.

Cloward, R. A. (1959). Illegitimate means, anomie, and deviant behavior. *American Sociological Review, 24*(2), 164-176.

Coker, A.L., Smith, P.H., Thompson, M.P., McKeown, R.E., Bethea, L., & Davis, K.E. (2002). Social support protects against the negative effects of partner violence on mental health. *Journal of Women's Health and Gender-Based Medicine, 11*(5), 465-476.

Conger, R. D., Elder, G. H., Lorenz, F. O., Conger, K. J., Simons, R. L., Whitbeck, L. B., et al. (1990). Linking economic hardship to marital quality and instability. *Journal of Marriage and the Family, 52*(3), 643-656.

DeMaris, A. A., Benson, M. L., Fox, G. L., Hill, T., & Van Wyk, J. (2003). Distal and proximal factors in domestic violence: A test of an integrated model. *Journal of Marriage and the Family, 65*, 652-667.

DeMaris, A. A., & Kaukinen, C. (2005). Violent victimization and women's mental and physical health: Evidence from a national sample. *Journal of Research in Crime and Delinquency, 42*(4), 384-411.

Denham, A.C., Frasier, P.Y., Hooten, E.G., Belson, L., Newton, W., Gonzalez, P., Begum, M., & Campbell, M.K. (2007). Intimate partner violence among Latinas in eastern North Carolina. *Violence Against Women, 13*(2), 123-140.

Desmond, S. A., & Kubrin, C. E. (2009). The power of place: Immigrant communities and adolescent violence. *Sociological Quarterly, 50*, 581-607.

Dhaher, E., Mikolajczk, R.T., Maxwell, A.E., & Kramer, A. (2010). Attitudes toward wife beating among Palestinian women of reproductive age from three cities in West Bank. *Journal of Interpersonal Violence, 25*, 518-537.

Dobash, R. E., & Dobash, R. P. (1979). *Violence against wives: A case against the patriarchy.* New York: Free Press.

Dobash, R. P., Dobash, R. E., Wilson, M., & Daly, M. (1992). The myth of sexual symmetry in marital violence. *Social Problems, 39*(1), 71-91.

Durose, M. R., Harlow, C. W., Langan, P. A., Motivans, M., Rantala, R. R., Smith, E. L., Constantin, E. (2005). *Family violence statistics: Including statistics on strangers and acquaintances* (No. NCJ-207846). Washington, DC: Bureau of Justice Statistics.

Earls, F. J., Brooks-Gunn, G., Raudenbush, S. W., & Sampson, R. J. (2002). Project on Human Development in Chicago Neighborhoods (PHDCN): Wave 1: Ann Arbor, MI: Inter-university Consortium for Political and Social Research, Grant 93-IJ-CX-K005.

Eng, S., Li, Y., Mulsow, M., & Fischer, J. (2010). Domestic violence against women in Cambodia: Husband's control, frequency of spousal discussion, and domestic violence reported by Cambodian women. *Journal of Family Violence, 25*, 237-246.

Feldman, C. M., & Ridley, C. A. (2000). The role of conflict-based communication responses and outcomes in male domestic violence toward female partners. *Journal of Social and Personal Relationships, 17*(4-5), 552-573.

Gelles, R. J. (1991). Physical violence, child abuse, and child homicide: A continuum of violence or distinct behaviors? *Human Nature, 2*(1), 59-72.

Gelles, R. J., & Straus, M. A. (1988). *Intimate violence: The definitive study of the causes and consequences of abuse in the American family*. New York: Simon and Schuster.

Gibson, C.L., Sullivan, C.J., Jones, S., & Piquero, A. (2010). "Does it take a village?" Assessing neighborhood influences on children's self-control. *Journal of Research in Crime and Delinquency, 47*(1), 31-62.

Goode, W. J. (1971). Force and violence in the family. *Journal of Marriage and the Family, 33*(4), 624-636.

Gottfredson, M. R., & Hirschi, T. (1990). *A general theory of crime*. Stanford: Stanford University Press.

Granovetter, M.S. (1973). Strength of weak ties. *American Sociological Review, 78*, 1360-1380.

Hadeed, L.F., & El-Bassel, N. (2006). Social support among Afro-Trinidadian women experiencing intimate partner violence. *Violence Against Women, 12*(8), 740-760.

Hipp, J.R., Tita, G.E., & Boggess, L.N. (2009). Intergroup and intragroup violence: Is violent crime an expression of group conflict or social disorganization? *Criminology, 47*(2), 521-564.

Hirschi, T., & Gottfredson, M. R. (1983). Age and the explanation of crime. *American Journal of Sociology, 89*, 552-584.

Holt, S., Buckley, H., & Whelan, S. (2008). The impact of exposure to domestic violence on children and young people: A review of the literature. *Child Abuse & Neglect, 32*, 979-810.

Holtzworth-Munroe, A., Bates, L., Smutzler, N., & Sandin, E. (1997). A brief review of the research on husband violence: Part I: Martially violent versus nonviolent men. *Aggression and Violent Behavior, 2*(1), 65-99.

Holtzworth-Munroe, A., Smutzler, N., & Bates, L. (1997). A brief review of the research on husband violence: Part III: Sociodemographic factors,

References

relationship factors, and differing consequences of husband and wife violence. *Aggression and Violent Behavior, 2*(3), 285-307.

Holtzworth-Munroe, A., Smutzler, N., & Sandin, E. (1997). A brief review of the research on husband violence: Part II: The psychological effects of husband violence on battered women and their children. *Aggression and Violent Behavior, 2*(2), 179-213.

Holtzworth-Munroe, A., & Stuart, G. L. (1994). Typologies of male batterers: Three subtypes and the differences among them. *Psychological Bulletin, 116*(3), 476-497.

Hunnicutt, G. (2009). Varieties of patriarchy and violence against women: Resurrecting "patriarchy" as a theoretical tool. *Violence Against Women, 15*(5), 553-573.

Johnson, M. P. (1995). Patriarchal terrorism and common couple violence: Two forms of violence against women. *Journal of Marriage and the Family, 57*, 283-294.

Johnson, M. P., & Ferraro, K. J. (2000). Research on domestic violence in the 1990s: Making decisions. *Journal of Marriage and the Family, 62*, 948-963.

Kasarda, J. D., & Janowitz, M. (1974). Community attachment in mass society. American *Sociological Review, 39*(3), 328-339.

Kaufman Kantor, G., & Straus, M. A. (1987). The "drunken bum" theory of wife beating. *Social Problems, 34*(3), 213-230.

Kilpatrick, D. G., Acierno, R., Resnick, H. S., Saunders, B. E., & Best, C. L. (1997). A 2-year longitudinal analysis of the relationships between violent assault and substance use in women. *Journal of Consulting and Clinical Psychology, 65*(5), 834-847.

Koening, M. A., Stephenson, R., Ahmed, S., Jejeebhoy, S. J., & Campbell, J. (2006). Individual and contextual determinants of domestic violence in north India. *American Journal of Public Health, 96*(1), 132-138.

Kornhauser, R. (1978). *Social sources of delinquency: An appraisal of analytic models.* Chicago: University of Chicago Press.

Krivo, L. J., & Peterson, R. D. (1996). Extremely disadvantaged neighborhoods and urban crime. *Social Forces, 75*(2), 619-648.

Kubrin, C. E., & Stewart, E. A. (2006). Predicting who reoffends: The neglected role of neighborhood context in recidivism studies. *Criminology, 44*(1), 165-197.

Kubrin, C. E., & Weitzer, R. (2003a). New directions in social disorganization theory. *Journal of Research in Crime and Delinquency, 40*(4), 374-402.

Kubrin, C. E., & Weitzer, R. (2003b). Retaliatory homicide: Concentrated disadvantage and neighborhood culture. *Social Problems, 50*(2), 157-180.

Lauritsen, J. L. (2001). The social ecology of violent victimization: Individual and contextual effects in the NCVS. *Journal of Quantitative Criminology, 17*(1), 3-32.

Lauritsen, J. L., & Schaum, R. J. (2004). The social ecology of violence against women. *Criminology, 42*(2), 323-357.

Lauritsen, J. L., & White, N. A. (2001). Putting violence in its place: The influence of race, ethnicity, gender, and place on the risk for violence. *Criminology and Public Policy, 1*(1), 37-60.

Lee, M.T., Martinez, R.Jr., & Rosenfeld, R. (2001). Does immigration increase homicide? Negative evidence from three border cities. *Sociological Quarterly, 42*, 559-580.

Li, Q., Kirby, R. S., Sigler, R. T., Hwang, S.-S., LaGory, M., & Goldenberg, R. L. (2010). A multilevel analysis of individual, household, and neighborhood correlates of intimate partner violence among low-income pregnant women in Jefferson County, Alabama. *American Journal of Public Health, 100*(3), 531-539.

Lily, J. R., Cullen, F. T., & Ball, R. A. (2002). *Criminological theory: Context and consequences* (3rd ed.). Thousand Oaks: Sage.

Lockhart, L. L. (1987). A reexamination of the effects of race and social class on the incidence of marital violence: A search for reliable differences. *Journal of Marriage and the Family, 49*(3), 603-610.

Lowenkamp, C. T., Cullen, F. T., & Pratt, T. C. (2003). Replicating Sampson and Groves's test of social disorganization theory: Revisiting a criminological classic. *Journal of Research in Crime and Delinquency, 40*(4), 351-373.

Lussier, P., Farrington, D.P., & Moffitt, T.E. (2009). Is the antisocial child the father of the abusive man? A 40-year prospective longitudinal study of the developmental antecedents of intimate partner violence. *Criminology, 47*(3), 741-780.

MacMillian, R., & Gartner, R. (1999). When she brings home the bacon: Labor-force participation and the risk of spousal violence against women. *Journal of Marriage and the Family, 61*(4), 947-958.

References

Magdol, L., Moffitt, T. E., Caspi, A., & Silva, P. A. (1998). Developmental antecedents of partner abuse: A prospective-longitudinal study. *Journal of Abnormal Psychology, 107*(3), 375-389.

Maimon, D., & Browning, C.R. (2010). Unstructured socializing, collective efficacy, and violent behavior among urban youth. *Criminology, 48*(2), 443-474.

Martinez, R. J., & Lee, M. T. (2000). Comparing the context of immigrant homicides in Miami: Haitians, Jamaicans, and Mariels. *International Migration Review, 34*(3), 794-812.

Martinez, R. J., Lee, M. T., & Nielsen, A. L. (2004). Segmented assimilation, local context and determinants of drug violence in Miami and San Diego: Does ethnicity and immigration matter? *International Migration Review, 38*(1), 131-157.

Mazerolle, L., Wickes, R., & McBroom, J. (2010). Community variations in violence: The role of social ties and collective efficacy in comparative context. *Journal of Research in Crime and Delinquency, 47*(1), 3-30.

Mazerolle, P., Maahs, J., & Bachman, R. (2000). Exposure to violence in the family: Unpacking the linkages to intimate partner violence. In G. L. Fox & M. L. Benson (Eds.), *Contemporary perspectives in family research: Families, crime and criminal justice* (Vol. 2, pp. 45-71). New York: Elsevier Science Inc.

McCann, I. L., Sakheim, D. K., & Abrahamson, D. J. (1988). Trauma and victimization: A model of psychological adaptation. *The Counseling Psychologist, 16*(4), 531-594.

Merton, R. K. (1938). Social structure and anomie. *American Sociological Review, 3*(5), 672-682.

Miles-Doan, R. (1998). Violence between spouses and intimates: Does neighborhood context matter? *Social Forces, 77*(2), 623-645.

Moe, A.M. (2007). Silenced voices and structured survival: Battered women's help seeking. *Violence Against Women, 13*(7), 676-699.

Morenoff, J. D., Sampson, R. J., & Raudenbush, S. W. (2001). Neighborhood inequality, collective efficacy, and the spatial dynamics of urban violence. *Criminology, 39*(3), 517-559.

O'Campo, P., Gielen, A. C., Faden, R. R., Xue, X., Kass, N., & Wang, M.C. (1995). Violence by male partners against women during the childbearing year: A contextual analysis. *American Journal of Public Health, 85*(8), 1092-1097.

Park, R. E., & Burgess, E. W. (1924). *Introduction to the science of sociology* (2nd ed.). Chicago: University of Chicago Press.

Pattillo, M. E. (1998). Sweet mothers and gangbangers: Managing crime in a black middle-class neighborhood. *Social Forces, 76*(3), 747-774.

Plass, P. S. (1993). African American family homicide: Patterns in partner, parent, and child victimization, 1985-1987. *Journal of Black Studies, 23*(4), 515-538.

Portes, A. (1998). Social capital: Its origins and applications in modern sociology. *Annual Review of Sociology, 24*, 1-24.

Pratt, T., & Cullen, F. T. (2005). Assessing the relative effects of macro-level predictors of crime: A meta-analysis. In M. Tonry (Ed.), *Crime and justice: A review of research* (Vol. 32, pp. 37-50). Chicago: University of Chicago Press.

Putnam, R. D. (2000). *Bowling alone: The collapse and revival of American community.* New York: Simon & Schuster.

Raudenbush, S. W., & Bryk, A. S. (2002). *Hierarchical linear models: Applications and data analysis methods* (2nd ed.). Thousand Oaks, CA: Sage.

Raudenbush, S. W., Bryk, A. S., Cheong, Y. F., Congdon, R., & Toit, M. D. (2004). *HLM 6: Hierarchical linear and nonlinear modeling.* Lincolnwood, IL: Scientific Software International, Inc.

Raudenbush, S. W., & Sampson, R. J. (1999). Ecometrics: Toward a science of assessing ecological settings, with application to the systematic social observation of neighborhoods. *Sociological Methodology, 29*, 1-41.

Ridley, C. A., & Feldman, C. M. (2003). Female domestic violence toward male partners: Exploring conflict responses and outcomes. *Journal of Family Violence, 18*(3), 157-170.

Rose, D. R., & Clear, T. R. (1998). Incarceration, social capital, and crime: Implications for social disorganization theory. *Criminology, 36*(3), 441-480.

Ross, C.E., & Mirowsky, J. (2009). Neighborhood disorder, subjective alienation, and distress. *Journal of Health and Social Behavior, 50*, 49-64.

Ross, C. E., Mirowsky, J., & Pribesh, S. (2001). Powerlessness and the amplification of threat: Neighborhood disadvantage, disorder, and mistrust. *American Sociological Review, 66*(4), 568-591.

References

Sampson, R. J. (1988). Local friendships ties and community attachment in mass society: A multilevel systemic model. *American Sociological Review, 53*(5), 766-779.

Sampson, R. J. (2006). Collective efficacy theory: Lessons learned and directions for future research. In F. T. Cullen, J. P. Wright & K. R. Blevins (Eds.), *Taking stock: The status of criminological theory - Advances in criminological theory* (Vol. 15, pp. 149-167). New Brunswick, NJ: Transaction.

Sampson, R.J. (2008). Rethinking crime and immigration. *Contexts, 7*(1), 28-33.

Sampson, R. J., & Bartusch, D. J. (1998). Legal cynicism and (subcultural?) tolerance of deviance: The neighborhood context of racial differences. *Law & Society Review, 32*(4), 777-804.

Sampson, R. J., & Bean, L. (2006). Cultural mechanisms and killing fields: A revised theory of community-level racial inequality. In R. D. Peterson, L. J. Krivo & J. Hagan (Eds.), *The many colors of crime: Inequalities of race, ethnicity, and crime in America* (pp. 8-35). New York: New York University Press.

Sampson, R. J., & Groves, W. B. (1989). Community structure and crime: Testing social disorganization theory. *The American Journal of Sociology, 94*(4), 774-802.

Sampson, R. J., & Laub, J. H. (1993). *Crime in the making: Pathways and turning points through life*. Cambridge: Harvard University Press.

Sampson, R. J., Morenoff, J. D., & Earls, F. (1999). Beyond social capital: Spatial dynamics of collective efficacy for children. *American Sociological Review, 64*, 633-660.

Sampson, R. J., Morenoff, J. D., & Gannon-Rowley, T. (2002). Assessing "neighborhood effects": Social processes and new directions in research. *Annual Review of Sociology, 28*, 443-478.

Sampson, R. J., Morenoff, J. D., & Raudenbush, S. W. (2005). Social anatomy of racial and ethnic disparities in violence. *American Journal of Public Health, 95*, 224-232.

Sampson, R. J., & Raudenbush, S. W. (1999). Systematic social observation of public spaces: A new look at disorder in urban neighborhoods. *American Journal of Sociology, 105*(3), 603-651.

Sampson, R. J., Raudenbush, S. W., & Earls, F. (1997). Neighborhoods and violent crime: A multilevel study of collective efficacy. *Science, 277*(5328), 918-924.

Sampson, R. J., & Wilson, W. J. (1995). Toward a theory of race, crime, and urban inequality. In J. Hagan & R. D. Peterson (Eds.), *Crime and inequality* (pp. 37-54). Stanford, CA: Stanford University Press.

Sellin, T. (1938). *Culture, conflict, and crime.* New York: Social Science Research Council.

Shaw, C. R., & McKay, H. D. (1942). *Juvenile delinquency and urban areas: A study of rates of delinquency in relation to differential characteristics of local communities in American cities.* Chicago: University of Chicago Press.

Sherman, L. W., & Berk, R. A. (1984). The specific deterrent effects of arrest for domestic assault. *American Sociological Review, 49*(2), 261-272.

Shihadeh, E. S., & Flynn, N. (1996). Segregation and crime: The effect of black social isolation on the rates of black urban violence. *Social Forces, 74*(4), 1235-1352.

Silver, E., & Miller, L. L. (2004). Sources of informal social control in Chicago neighborhoods. *Criminology, 42*(3), 551-583.

Stets, J. E. (1991). Cohabiting and marital aggression: The role of social isolation. *Journal of Marriage and the Family, 53*(3), 669-680.

Stewart, E. A., & Simons, R. L. (2006). Structure and culture in African American adolescent violence: A partial test of the "code of the street" thesis. *Justice Quarterly, 23*(1), 1-33.

Stewart, E.A., & Simons, R.L. (2010). Race, code of the street, and violent delinquency: A multilevel investigation of neighborhood street culture and individual norms of violence. *Criminology, 48*(2), 569-605.

Stith, S. M., Smith, D. B., Penn, C. E., Ward, D. B., & Tritt, D. (2004). Intimate partner physical abuse perpetration and victimization risk factors: A meta-analytic review. *Aggression and Violent Behavior, 10*, 65-98.

Straus, M. A. (1979). Measuring intrafamily conflict and violence: The Conflict Tactics (CT) Scales. *Journal of Marriage and the Family, 41*(1), 75-88.

Straus, M. A., Gelles, R. J., & Steinmetz, S. K. (2006). *Behind closed doors: Violence in the American family.* New Brunswick: Transaction.

Straus, M. A., Hamby, S. L., Boney-McCoy, S., & Sugarman, D. B. (1996). The revised Conflict Tactics Scale (CTS2). *Journal of Family Issues, 17*(3), 283-316.

References

Sugarman, D. B., & Frankel, S. L. (1996). Patriarchal ideology and wife-assault: A meta-analytic review. *Journal of Family Violence, 11*(1), 13-40.

Sutherland, E. H., & Cressey, D. R. (1978). *Criminology* (10th ed.). Philadelphia: Lippincott.

Szinovacz, M. E., & Egley, L. C. (1995). Comparing one-partner and couple data on sensitive marital behaviors: The case of marital violence. *Journal of Marriage and the Family, 57*(4), 995-1010.

Thompson, M. P., & Kingree, J. B. (2006). The roles of victim and perpetrator alcohol use in intimate partner violence outcomes. *Journal of Interpersonal Violence, 21*(2), 163-177.

Tjaden, P., & Thoennes, N. (1998). *Prevalence, incidence, and consequences of violence against women: Findings from the National Violence Against Women Survey.* (No. NCJ-172837). Washington, DC: Department of Justice, National Institute of Justice.

Tjaden, P., & Thoennes, N. (2000). Prevalence and consequences of male-to-female and female-to-male intimate partner violence as measured by the National Violence Against Women Survey. *Violence Against Women, 6*(2), 142-161.

Van Wyk, J., Benson, M. L., Fox, G. L., & DeMaris, A. A. (2003). Detangling individual-, partner-, and community-level correlates of partner violence. *Crime and Delinquency, 49*(3), 412-438.

Veysey, B. M., & Messner, S. F. (1999). Further testing of social disorganization theory: An elaboration of Sampson and Groves's "Community structure and crime". *Journal of Research in Crime and Delinquency, 36*(2), 156-174.

Voydanoff, P. (1990). Economic distress and family relations: A review of the eighties. *Journal of Marriage and the Family, 52*(4), 1099-1115.

Warner, B. D. (2003). The role of attenuated culture in social disorganization theory. *Criminology, 41*(1), 73-97.

Warner, B. D., & Pierce, G. L. (1993). Reexamining social disorganization theory using calls to the police as a measure of crime. *Criminology, 31*(4), 493-517.

Warner, B. D., & Wilcox Rountree, P. (1997). Local social ties in a community and crime model: Questioning the systemic nature of informal social control. *Social Problems, 44*(4), 520-536.

Wellman, B. & Wortley, S. (1990). Different strokes from different folks: Community ties and social support. *American Journal of Sociology, 96*, 558-588.

White, H. R., & Widom, C. S. (2003). Intimate partner violence among abused and neglected children in young adulthood: The mediating effects of early aggression, antisocial personality, hostility and alcohol problems. *Aggressive Behavior, 29*, 332-345.

Widom, C. S. (1989). Does violence beget violence? A critical examination of the literature. *Psychological Bulletin, 106*(1), 3-28.

Wilcox Rountree, P., & Warner, B. D. (1999). Social ties and crime: Is the relationship gendered? *Criminology, 37*(4), 789-814.

Wilkinson, D. L. (2007). Local social ties and willingness to intervene: Textured views among violent urban youth of neighborhood social control dynamics and situations. *Justice Quarterly, 24*(2), 185-220.

Wilkinson, D. L., & Hamerschlag, S. J. (2005). Situational determinants in intimate partner violence. *Aggression and Violent Behavior, 10*, 333-361.

Wilson, J. Q., & Kelling, G. (1982). The police and neighborhood safety: Broken windows. *Atlantic, 127*, 29-38.

Wilson, W. J. (1987). *The truly disadvantaged: The inner city, the underclass, and public policy.* Chicago: University of Chicago Press.

Wolfgang, M. E., & Ferracuti, F. (1967). *The subculture of violence: Towards an integrated theory in criminology.* London: Tavistock.

Wooldredge, J. D., Griffin, T., & Pratt, T. (2001). Considering hierarchical models for research on inmate behavior: Predicting misconduct with multilevel data. *Justice Quarterly, 18*(1), 203-231.

Wright, E.M., & Benson, M.L. (2010). Immigration and intimate partner violence: Exploring the immigrant paradox. *Social Problems, 57*(3), 480-503.

Xie, M., & McDowall, D. (2008). The effects of residential turnover on household victimization. *Criminology, 46* (3), 539-575.

Yllo, K., & Straus, M. A. (1981). Interpersonal violence among married and cohabiting couples. *Family Relations, 30*(3), 339-347.

Yount, K.M. (2005). Resources, family organization, and domestic violence against married women in Minya, Egypt. *Journal of Marriage and Family, 67*, 579-596.

Yount, K.M., & Li, L. (2009). Women's "justification" of domestic violence in Egypt. *Journal of Marriage and Family, 71*, 1125-1140.